"*I hold the Guinness Record for writing 40,000 jokes. Beth Schaefer has put more than that in one book...and I think she may have more funny ones.*"

~Joe Martin

American Cartoonist (Washington Post's "Mr. Boffo", "Willy n' Ethel")

Contents:

1. **The Nutty Years of the Jon Stewart Presidency in a Nutshell**
   This is a "term paper" by Edison Bell—a fictional college student at Lake Forest College in Illinois.
   This term paper appears in *Grade A Papers: The Slap Stack—A Funny Coffee Table Book for English Teachers and the Universe*. *Grade A Papers* contains 30 funny fake student papers; 4 hilarious composition theorist parodies; and over 30 diverse, custom-designed illustrations and graphics from artists across the world.

2. **The Nutty Years of the Jon Stewart Presidency in a Nutshell "Cheep Sheet"**

3. **Make No Room for Kids: Bells Ding for Online Classes K-8**
   An Argumentative Abstract by Richard Fukerson
   This is a parody of composition theorist Richard Fulkerson. It appears in *Grade A Papers: The Slap Stack—A Funny Coffee Table Book for English Teachers and the Universe*. Other theorists parodied in *Grade A Papers: The Slap Stack* include Peter Elbow (Peter Ankle), David Bartholomae (David Barfholomae), and Anne Lamott (Anne Lamott Applesauce).

4. **My Flesh is My Blanket Inside which I Hide**
   This fake student's (Simon Simon) paper will be featured in *Grade A Papers II: A Funny Coffee Table Book for History Teachers and the Universe*. [Release slated 2015.] *Grade A Papers II* and all following *Grade A Papers* books will take place at the imaginary Whimsor College in Columbia, Missouri.

Drop by booksonawhim.com to learn about the *Grade A Papers* series, purchase a funny coffee table book, or browse the Whimsor College University online portal.

Books on a Whim
take pen and fly merry
www.booksonawhim.com

Written by Beth Schaefer

Copyright © 2014, All Rights Reserved
Books on a Whim (Evanston)

ISBN: 978-0-578-15202-8

This term paper is dedicated to my A-list sister, Jenny.
I love you, hermana.

The Nutty Years of the Jon Stewart Presidency in a Nutshell
Featuring: The Presidents Playhouse

Table of Cornnuts

Part I

OBAMA RESIGNS TO HAWAII
- Obama Brushes off Birth Certificate
- The First Lady Thrusts

A RESURRECTED ELECTION
- Republican Primary
- Democratic Primary
- The Zeppo Marx Roast

ART AND MONEY: CHAMPAGNE FINANCE
- Chicago Billionaires OutsmArt Chicago Mayor
- Chicago Mayor OutsmArts Chicago Billionaires

THE DEBATES
- Mount Rushmore Face-Off
- A Staged Debate
  - Ryan Regresses

STEWART'S INAUGURATION AND EXECUTIVE OUTFIT
- The Assassination Attempt and the Spaceballs Alien
- Colbert's Silent Tongue
- Stewart's Cabinet Unhinged
  - SOS!
  - Second Class Secretaries
- Samantha's Bees and John's Olives
- The Incorporation of Congress and the Inferiority Complex of the SEC

Part II

ROMANTIC ESCAPADES AND THE NSA
- The Sexting Scandal of Petraeus and Paula
- E-Dating Hackers Spread Virus

GLOBAL FRICTION AND OTHER TALES OF DISASTER
- The Amazon Plant Invasion
- An Infestation of Tics Down Under
- McDonalds Serves Freedom Flies
- The Study Abroad Tax Evasion Scandal
- The Clothing of Guantanamo
- Italy Loses Color
- The Controversial Erection of the BOLLYWOOD Sign in Tirumala

Part III

DOMESTICATED NUISANCES AND A CRAZY LITTLE THING CALLED WAR
- Giving America the New Bird
- Fraggles Fuss about Fracking
- The Mississippi Missile Crisis
- A Crockpot of Bull and the Texas Secession
- The Perfume Wars

HEALTH AND EPIDEMICS
- The Whore on Drugs
- The Regeneration of the Smartphone into the Human Hand
- The Long Term Effects of Lasik Come to Light

AN ECONOMIC COLLAPSE AND ITS NIPPLE EFFECT
- The Rise and Fall of the White Bread Factory: Cutting off the Trust
- Obama-Éclair (The Affordable Heath-Bar Act) and the Smithsonian Sweet Tooth
  - Three Years in the Running
  - Form and Sustenance
  - A Moveable Sweet

Part IV

THE PRESIDENTS PLAYHOUSE
- The White House is a Fun House: From Remote Control Drones to "Being John Edwards"
- The Presidents Playhouse: A Cellar Discovery
- Life After Laughs

Edison Bell
Composition Class
Lake Forest College
Professor Edward Schaefer

Summer 2016
Term Paper

The Nutty Years of the Jon Stewart Presidency in a Nutshell

(2012-2016)

PART I

OBAMA RESIGNS TO HAWAII

Obama Brushes off Birth Certificate

No American citizen or undocumented immigrant will forget the stupefying discovery of former President **Barack Obama'** *Certificate of Naissance*.

Who could have guessed that forensic archeologists on a transpolar treasure hunt would unearth a flimsy rectangular document, its frozen watermark preserved. With the deployment of a protractor, ice pick and tweezers, the scientists plucked the certificate in its pristine state.

While point of conception is debatable, Obama's birth did *not* take place in the state of Hawaii. His birth took place at geodetic latitude 90° North at the North Pole, which the scientists' treasure map pinpointed as the exact location of Santa's dismantled Workshop.

Obama's birth transpired long before Santa's Workshop was procured by K-Mart Corporation in the infamous acquisition of 1987 before their "Blue Light Specials" went LED.

The Obama Administration denied the authenticity of the snowy certificate. They brushed it off as some prop planted for a reality show like "The Amazing Race" or "The Apprentice."

But the FBI (Federal Bureau of Insinuators) flew in a medium who substantiated that Obama, indeed, was born in Santa's Workshop.

The medium affirmed, "I sense his presents." Polarized by the public, a despondent Obama withdrew from office.

However, he made a symbolic gesture in 2013 by moving to Hawaii to shoot hoops and skeet. Obama founded HULA (The Hungry Unicorns Live Association), a non-profit that raises funds and educates people on the existence and famine of unicorns.

booksonawhim.com

The First Lady Thrusts

Obama's wife, former first lady **Michelle**, kept her presence public too. After the North Pole fiasco, Mrs. Obama drew awareness and crowds to her new fitness campaign: A revival of **Jane Fonda's** popular 1982 exercise videotape "Workout."

Mrs. Obama introduced "Workout" to middle schools to bolster fitness and herald the historical significance of the VHS. Schools across the nation mandatorily integrated "Workout" into their gym programs.

Conservatives were majorly P.E.-ed off, and didn't take it sitting down. Their allegation: Parents have the right to opt their kids out of gym class whenever the video plays. They cited the suggestive contortions of the "Buttocks Thrust"—Fonda reclined on her back, heaving her buttocks up and down—as corruptive.

Meanwhile, gym teachers (who bi-nature lean liberally) insisted their thrusts were innocent. "Students are strengthening their largest bipartisan muscle," was the gym teachers' unanimous rebuttal. "Both sides must support the other. We must not simply be fair-weather ends."

After a buddy battle, the Republicans' argument was deemed a tighter means to an end. Gym teachers admitted defeat, consoling themselves with lots of socks in sneakers.

A RESURRECTED ELECTION

Republicans did not claim victory, however, in the presidential battle of 2012—although both sides boasted formidable opponents.

On the right: **Santorum. Perry. Bachmann. Romney.** (Rumor had it **Sarah Palin** was planning to steak another slab at running, but these rumors proved ungrounded. Wary of reentering the spotlight, Palin moved to *behind-the-scenes* show business, accepting a role as **Laura Palmer's** speech coach in the 2014 revival of "Twin Peaks: Cooper Bobs for Answers.")

On the left: **Clinton. Clinton. Clooney. Stewart.** (Former Vice President **Joe Biden**, it's said, did not reflect upon a run as leading man.

When Obama resigned, Biden suffered a complex stemming back to his failed Democratic Primary run for President in '88 when he was caught plagiarizing **Dr. Seuss's** *Horton Hears a Who*. So, Biden chose not to run for president in '12, disappointing himself as a running mate hopeful.)

Republican Primary

Rick Santorum only lasted one month in the primaries due to his sickening trash talk. (He caught a bronchial infection while stumping at the town dump, and admitted himself into Der Zauberberg Sanatorium in Switzerland for convalescence.)

Rick Perry did not last much longer. Perry was removed from the ballot on the grounds of his unknown geographical whereabouts. Investigators confirm, however, that Perry is alive and well and living in 4414 BC.

The last time Perry was seen by modern man was March 2, 2012. He was boarding a time machine at Cape Canaveral, making a bold move to travel back in time to substantiate Creationism. Perry, the sole passenger on "Flight H.G. Well-Why-Not," evaporated with his vessel at launch.

Mrs. Anita Perry received a postcard on July 4, 2012 that read: "Hee haw! This is unf***ing-believable. It's like fireworks down here every single night with pistols, pagans, pushies, pullies, and all kinds of crazy s**t. And there are no f***ing monkeys, eat that Dems. Miss you babe, Your Perr-Bear." On the front: a photo of a Piña Colada against a sunset with "Wish you were beer!" written in cursive.

And so the Republican Primary fizzled down to a heated friendly fire between two.

Michelle Bachmann yearned to become the first Woman president. **Mitt Romney** aspired to become the first Mormon president.

He lashed out that putting the "fe" before the "male" is like putting the tart before the horse. Bachmann lashed back that Mormons were Muslims that got the vowels wrong.

But Romney wouldn't have the alphabetical fuss he feared.

On May 7, 2012, Bachmann had an epiphany. She awoke at 6:00 a.m. to **Limbaugh's** light, lilting lungs on KTCN-AM. She showered; slipped into her ironed slacks; sipped her hot, freshly brewed coffee; and pressed on to read *The Telegraph* awaiting her on the kitchen counter.

The headline: "Paeleoclimatological research claims dinosaur flatulence may have warmed the earth (and extinguished the species)" (*Current Biology*, Vol. 21, Iss. 9). Bachmann spilled her scalding coffee upon her slacks.

The shock of extinction by odor, she later reported, impressed upon her an awareness that it stinks life is short.

"Life is a gas that can pass in a blast," she explained, simultaneously pulling out of the race and her finger. The dinosaur discovery prompted the consummation of her true calling: concert pianist in drag.

And then there was won.

Delighted by his good fortune ($250 MM) Romney took center stage in July 2012 as winner of the Republican Primary. He seemed a surefire success! That is, until the infamous controversy over his 47¢ tip at TGI Fridays (West Boca Raton).

On September 17, 2012, a secretly-filmed video surfaced and went vinyl. In it, Romney brags that he tipped a Friday's waitress just 47¢ for a $10 bill.

"Waitresses are not entitled to tips," he stated, continuing on to claim he has "menus full of waitresses perfectly happy to work for minimum wage alone" and "outstanding support to push the tipping infrastructure off its legs to topple."

At first Romney defended his tip, but upon pressure from the Association of Waitress Elite Legion's Committee of Ordinary Meal Extravagance (AWELCOME) he later claimed he miscalculated 20%.

But the humiliation became too hot to handle after **Clint Eastwood** whispered sweet nothings to an empty chair on the stage of the Republican National Convention in Tampa, and so Romney stepped off.

Democratic Primary

It was no surprise when **Hillary Clinton** declared her candidacy for POTUS in 2008. And—despite the fact she was challenging her employer—she reentered the primary in 2012.

Republicans had no qualms about digging up a little dirt on her. They found their dirt in Clinton's '08 campaign TV commercial: "It's 3 a.m. and your children are fast asleep. But there's a phone in the White House, and it's ringing. Something's happening. Who do you want answering the phone?"

In '12 Clinton repeatedly *re*ran this same commercial. The re-airing of Clinton's ad unnerved President Obama (then still thought to be Hawaiian). He was so distressed that he went on a three-week bender at Martha's Vineyard.

After his splendor bender, a sober Obama disclosed that he had received threatening phone calls at 3 a.m. throughout his four years as president, and the eerie '08 commercial triggered his spree.

This prompted a young defense contractor in Hawaii to investigate. DNA (Do Not Ask) evidence and a *Verizon Wiredlist* revealed that Hillary Clinton *herself* had been prank calling Obama. Here's how:

When Clinton was appointed Secretary of State in '09, her New Hire packet included Obama's bedroom landline # in its print directory. And so, thinking connivingly ahead to the 2012 election, Clinton routinely dialed the president from an unlisted number—exercising a variety of phonetic techniques to terrify the poor man.

Her repertoire included heavy breathing; speaking in tongues; operatic warm-up scales; invitations to "play a nice game of Solitaire"; the query "have you checked the children?"; and a fine assortment of assassination threats—from slaying by spork to murder by wedgie.

Hillary Clinton withdrew from the 2012 race and switched to AT&T (which shortly thereafter was acquired by Verizon).

But there was another Clinton in the race. Hillary and **Bill's daughter Chelsea** stepped into her mother's shoes to run in her place but get somewhere. (Her mother campaigned for Chelsea, but was prohibited from making fundraising calls.)

Yet Chelsea's political interests hit a yellow brick wall when she married investment banker **JP Morgan Jr.** on July 31.

Now a matron with duties to look after, she left the race and moved on up to a deluxe apartment in the sky. Chelsea's philanthropic interests remained intact and she opened a soup kitchen in her $10.5 MM Manhattan condominium.

The savviest player in the '12 Democratic Primary was limousine liberal and leading ladies man **George Clooney**. He had the broads' backing and the support of the biggest names in Hollywood: From **Kevin Bacon** to **Tom Hanks** to **Leonardo DiCaprio** to **Meryl Streep** to **John Lithgow** and back to **Kevin Bacon**.

But Clooney Fever didn't last long. On Monday, August 13, 2012, an LA bouncer at *Sky Zone* (1625 W. 190th St.) disclosed Hollywood's greatest-until-then-kept-secret: Clooney was a homosexual with a penchant for male models 30 years his junior.

The timing was ill; Clooney had *just* sworn heterosexuality on **Barbara Walters** one day prior to the leak. He risked penalty of perjury and going to the can! Then the damn burst to all well when DNAA (Do Not Ask Again) proved Clooney was the illegitimate child of **Cary Grant** and **Desi Arnez**.

Clooney abdicated his candidacy, citing interest in "The Facts of Life: The Film," in which he would play the handyman dressed as **Mrs. Garrett**.

America was left with one man commanding: **Jon Leibowitz Stewart**.

Under Stewart's reign, Comedy Central's "The Daily Show with Jon Stewart" garnered 18 Prime-Time Emmys and a Certificate of Merit from Spike T.V.'s Guys Choice Awards for being "a generally likable guy" and "someone you'd want to hang out with."

Most Americans assume that **Stephen Colbert** was Stewart's first pick as running mate. In actuality, Stewart first approached a conflicted **Colin Powell**. Powell deliberated over Stewart's offer, but declined in order to accept a judicial spot on "American Idol."

It was then Stewart tuned in to Colbert—an equally brilliant late night comic blessed with beady, extraterrestrial eyes.

The comedians knew each other well; Colbert used to serve as Stewart's squire on "The Daily Show" set and they had co-hosted the "Trash Cannes Awards" at the Oscars. (To quote former Illinois Governor **Rob Bragojevich**, the Stewart/Colbert ticket was so "f***ing golden" it could have been made by **Willy Wonka**.)

The Zeppo Marx Roast

While *almost* controversy-free, Stewart had one carry-on item of political baggage: The infamous Zeppo Marx Roast in '99. Stewart, then a fresh face on "The Daily Show," roasted his very first guest, a 98-year old **Zeppo Marx**, who was promoting his new book *Well, I Studied Comedic Dramatics at Vassar*.

Stewart, typically *commended* for his sardonic charm, verbally walloped the old actor, slamming Marx's "feeble attempts at romantic leads," "alarmingly unfunny deliveries," and pinpointing Marx's scenes as "the time when the audience ducks out of the theater to refill their popcorn buckets."

Flustered and crushed, Marx rose abruptly to leave, but tripped over his armchair—triggering uproarious laugher from the live audience who thought it part of the act. When it was later revealed the fall was NOT staged, former fans chastised Stewart, who they compared to **Michael Moore**. (In '02, Moore had distastefully interviewed a frail, disoriented **Charleston Heston** about his chew.)

Fortunately, in Zeppo Marx's case it had a happy ending. On "The Daily Show," Marx had gotten his biggest laugh ever, and by the end of the night he was beaming.

ART AND MONEY: CHAMPAGNE FINANCE

Chicago Billionaires OutsmArt Chicago Mayor

(Writer's Interlude: I mailed Grade A Papers: The Slap Stack with this version to Chicago billionaire Ken Griffin. Customizable books are a beauty of self-publishing! They didn't see Rahm Emanuel excerpt that follows or this interlude. - Beth)

The excavation of Obama's birth certificate in the North Pole crushed moochers across America. The news was particularly gutting to Democrats in Obama's hometown, Chicago.

A lamentably "blue" city, Chicago was its bluest upon Obama's resignation. It was especially devastating for the 240,000 supporters who had gathered at Grant Park in 2008 for Obama's victory speech.

Five years later, the same 240,000 crestfallen Democrats reassembled in July 2013 at the same spot during "The Taste of Chicago"—to commiserate over a hotdog and a beer. The crowd of masses arrived at Grant Park only to learn "The Taste" had moved to Wrigley Field—home to the Chicago Cubs (arch rival team to Obama's beloved White Sox).

While the self-entitled bemoaned Obama's resignation, the rich and beautiful celebrated. As the lot of Democrats wept over their imaginary beers in a vacant Grant Park, Republicans held a classy evening gala at the Chicago Art Institute's new modern wing. There was a sumptuous buffet with a pink champagne fountain centerpiece.

Chicago native and silver screen star **Vince Vaughn** served as Master of Ceremonies, unveiling new pieces of art to mark the occasion. These new pieces included **Henri Matisse's** "Sunburns by a River," **Jackson Pollock's** "Cracked Egg's Entrails," and **Man Ray's** "One Night in Bangkok Set."

The pinnacle of the party was the unveiling of two pristine life-size statues of **Ken and Anne Griffin**, the most beautiful billionaire couple *in the universe.*

The Griffin statues are draped in ivory-sculpted silk sheets and ornamented with sculpted swans swimming in a marble pond at the loved ones' smooth feet.

The statues—which stand hand-in-hand—grace Griffin Court on the first floor pavilion of the modern wing.

(The real Griffins, also philanthropists, charitably donated $19 million in '06 to the creation of the modern wing, which explains why the Art Institute makes the perfect home for the classical statues.)

By stark contrast, the Art Institute hosts a grotesque brass statue, which was relegated to the old wing in 2013 to make room for the gala.

The crooked statue is in the likeness of Chicago Mayor **Rahm Emanuel**, inarguably the nerdiest-looking Democrat in the City of Chicago. Unlike the Griffin statues—who were prudently garbed in elegant films of ivory—Emanuel was naked all but for a tiny green leaf of tin covering his groin.

Due to the drastic decrease in field trips—following Emanuel's closing of 49 Chicago public grade schools in 2013—the Emanuel statue is barely regarded.

Chicago Mayor OutsmArts Chicago Billionaires

*(Writer's Interlude: I mailed **Grade A Papers: The Slap Stack** with this version to Chicago Mayor Rahm Emanuel. Customizable books are a beauty of self-publishing. He didn't see Ken Griffin excerpt that precedes this or this interlude. - Beth)*

Following the excavation of Obama's birth certificate in the North Pole, Chicago Mayor **Rahm Emanuel**, former White House Chief of Staff, dived back into national politics in an effort to polish the image of the Democratic Party.

Chicago Democrats—always a rowdy, optimistic bunch—rallied with Emanuel in support of a Democratically-controlled Executive Branch. The same 240,000 Obama revelers who attended the '08 victory speech at Grant Park reassembled at U.S Raise-Hellular Field in October of 2013 to "Party plan."

In a jocular huddle, the likable-minded chose to crash the Republican fundraising event "Nightie Night." (Second City class Republicans had scheduled a sassy pajama gala at the Chicago Art Institute's new modern wing. "Nightie Night" touted **Ken Griffin**, Chicago billionaire and CEO of Citadel—a portable Wisconsin gas station—who was announcing a run for president.)

The museum curator went all out with catering, which included cured salami; clébard de poisson cher (swordfish mated with lobster); an assortment of skins of Camembert, Brie and Jell-O; hairy potato-sized truffles (fungi) to be eaten with chopsticks; and cherry tomato-sized truffles (chocolate) to be eaten with manicured pinkies.

Beverages included flutes of caviar smoothies and flights of oyster juice. The fountain centerpiece: Two mini-waterfalls of Charles Lafitte Rosé and Beaujolais cascading to a riptide that funneled into a glass ant farm basin. (The tide of cheap champagne and bad wine flushed in and out, back and forth through the tunnels of sand.)

Washed out actor **Vince Vaughn** was Master of Ceremonies. Vaughn unveiled a masterpiece to mark the occasion and adorn the modern wing.

It was the pinnacle of the party: two glass statues of Ken Griffin and his wife **Anne**—whom he met in 2003 at 872 North State Street just off the Red Line.

The billionaire twosome (or threesome when they brought their nanny into the mix) was acclaimed for their charitable ventures, which included buying the abstract oil painting "False Start" for their personal collection.

(They would later learn it was finger-painted by **Jasper Johns**, a 10-month old child from the Abrakadoodle Art Studio for Kids in Singapore.) For a mere $80 million, the frugal art lovers purchased "False Start," which hangs today above the lovers' gilded conscience.

In '06 the Griffins donated $19 million to the Art Institute for its new wing. The Griffin glass statues are nudes—the curves chipped in all the right spots.

When you position the statues *just so*, the sunlight reflecting off Lake Michigan ricochets into the gallery and shoots prisms across the couple's sensually opened mouths—as if they are eating air bubbles of rainbows.

The Griffin statues are adjoined at their rear ends like pygopagus twins—Anne's perked up slightly in mid-twerk. The statues are ornamented with glass cockatoos mating in a glass puddle at the Griffins' calloused feet.

Just as Vaughn uncovered the billionaires, the 240,000 Democrats crashed the bedding. The riot was helmed by Emanuel and avid Clinton (Hillary) supporter **Owen Wilson**.

Talk about anarchy at the Art Institute! There was pushing and punching. Kicking and screaming. Hair pulling and teasing. Tearing up floorboards and running with slivers.

Chicago celebrity **Oprah Winfrey**—who was fighting alongside Emanuel and Wilson—hoisted a giant gray bean off the buffet and *hurled* it at the glass ant farm. (In litigation later—the suit concerned the collateral damage of whole families—Winfrey claimed she had thought the bean was an innocuous cloud, incapable of insecticidal impact.)

The finely catered food—fresh and impartially digested—went flying in the air without owner.

Ultimately, the Democrats (in "Yes We Can United!" apparel) and the Republicans (in nighties *marching* with lucky liberated ants) clashed at the tip of the Ken statue's foremost cockatoo.

At this point, a now sickly salami—stuck to the ceiling—unclenched its sticky grip and splattered on Ken's head-given cockatoo—lubricating its stiffness with meat fat.

The greasy moisture and weighty bulk (the salami came from Costco) broke *3 billion shards into a puddle of glass*. (The Griffin statues remain on exhibit today, but the Ken statue's groin is prudently covered with a food stamp.)

The political pajama party was a bust, and the once hopeful Ken withdrew without further incident. The "Art Institute Riot" secured Emanuel's spot as a brave, no-nonsense leader.

Emanuel himself has hinted at a possible 2020 presidential run. "I will reveal my decision," Emanuel stated in '15, "at a place no man has ever been: The Smith Museum of Stained Glass Windows at Chicago's Navy Pier. *And,* I will boldly invite Winfrey as a gesture to symbolize how trust conquers fragility."

THE DEBATES

Mount Rushmore Face-Off

Flash back to the '08 election debates. Remember when **John McCain** called in sick with a grin ache? Well, Romney (then age 61) stepped in as Interim Debater to "take on" the ambitious young senator from Illinois. (Romney was not intimidated. He had revealed his acting chops in the Cranbrook School's rendition of "Hair" in 1963.) Romney figured if he won McCain the debate, he'd be a poster boy for 2012.

Obama was highly regarded as an eloquent speaker. It appeared a no-brainer that Obama would win the '08 debates, and subsequently, the presidency. It seemed *such a sure thing* that sculptors started carving Obama's face into Mount Rushmore—between **Thomas Jefferson** and **Theodore Roosevelt**.

The sculptors applied the "Sideism" technique, in which a sculpture is created vertically from left to right. (This method originated in the late 1950s—devised by a company of Venetian blinds artists gone rogue—who, of their own accord—regularly met on the side in the shade under the Bridge of Sides to hone their gills.)

Just before the first debate, the sculptors had completed 50% of the carving. The complete left half of Obama's face was finely sculpted.

To America's astonishment, during the 1st debate Obama entered a mysterious trance…rendered speechless. (Obama later explained he had been having a flashback to his pot-smoking daze and was picturing himself in a "white classmate's sparkling new van.")

Romney won the first debate, and everyone commended McCain on such a great job.

Panicked, the sculptors carved the right half of Romney's face into the granite—adjoining Obama's left. The finished (frankly frightening) face was christened "Romama."

In 2009, **Margo Lion**, co-chair of the president's Committee of Arts and Humanities (CAH), ordered a federal engineer to affix an enormous rope from behind Romama's ears that ties behind its head like a Halloween mask.

To this day, Lion insists it's a safety measure to keep the rock from falling. (But the vast populace believes it was a bipartisan attempt to save face.)

…Legend has it Jefferson and Roosevelt have edged slightly away from Romama's face—in fear or perhaps embarrassment.

A Staged Debate

Back to the 2012 election: Stewart takes it upon himself.

The U.S. Constitution's 39th Amendment (*Bill of Rights*, Appendix F) states that *a minimum of two* presidential debates must take place even if "there be-ith one sole man, standing alone, by himself, with no other, on his own, stag."

To satisfy this technicality, Stewart teamed up with Apple® to help him secure the job by undertaking the technical specs. So Apple® invented the nation's first "Online Town Hall Forum"—a program that yielded fruitful results.

The forum's moderator was the flirtatious voice of **Samantha from "Sex in the City."** (In 2010 Samantha also whored her voice as a Manhattan GPS orator—downloadable for $12.95.)

Online spectators voted for their winner by text *(standard text messaging rates may be waived)*, and Stewart won the debate by his lonesome by a landslide.

The second debate was a one-man show—"performance art" style format. It took place at the tiny, avant-garde Kraine Theater in Manhattan, and was moderated by performance artist **Laurie Anderson**.

Stewart—wearing black tights and a turtle neck—role-played *both* himself *and* his opponent. A soft white spotlight turned off and then on whenever he switched characters.

Stewart would have received a standing ovation if the poor theater's ceiling had been high enough. Republicans, however, stooped to complain it was a biased debate because Stewart enacted the world's most annoying persona—**Jar Jar Binks**— as his imaginary opponent.

Ryan Regresses

The '12 Vice Presidential debate was scheduled to air October 11 on ABC at 6 p.m. Pacific in Kentucky.

Veep nominee Colbert—freshly preened and powdered—slid his fingers through his hair and dampened his nape with gel. The sprucely clad candidate—a dapper 48-years young—chalked and fondled his hands in anticipatory eagerness to impel himself upon viewers.

Colbert was slotted to face off against then-Congressional Representative **Paul Ryan**, a whimper-snapper farm-boy from Spread Eagle, Wisconsin, where his mother **Betty** nursed him into politics.

But when the moderator, **Martha Radasstz**, beat the gong with her mallet, Ryan was nowhere to be weaned. Rumors ran rampant: Was Ryan not running? Was Ryan on the run? Did Ryan have the runs? Would Ryan return or relinquish his race?

Without even parting his lips, Colbert was awarded the win, left speechless in brazen bashfulness.

The next morning, a Republican search party—on a quest to save Ryan—located him in private. The congressman was in a tight corner, feverishly suckling a bottle of water. Ryan came clean and confessed his addiction to pure liquid hydrogen and oxygen—sapping his political future and tapping his mother's teat.

STEWART'S INAUGURATION AND EXECUTIVE OUTFIT

The Assassination Attempt and the Spaceballs Alien

On Monday, January 21, 2013 Jonathan "Stu" Leibowitz Stewart—aside his wife, **Tracey Big-MacShane** and ex-wife **Annie**—was sworn in as President of the United States.

The adrenaline-pumping part of the event was the shotgun assassination attempt on Stewart by a bow-tied, once 35-year old man on air. Stewart was caught in the crossfire, but saved by CNN executives who threw a towel in at the stumbling gunman, tripping up his aim. The would-be assassin was identified as **Tucker Carlson**.

Defense unsuccessfully argued that Carlson was just implementing his Daily task list in bullet points. But the judge didn't see it that day. Carlson was made to sit in the back row as punishment and deprived of sweets for a week.

Upon taking the motels.com-sponsored oath on a dresser drawer Bible, panic ensued over who would sing the National Anthem.

Janet Jackson had been slotted to perform, but Security stopped her at the metal detectors—citing a war-drone malfunction and frisking for proof (founded).

Fortunately, actor **John Hurt** was in inaugural attendance, and, as luck would have it, **the alien** who had made a cameo in **Mel Brooks'** "Spaceballs" (1987) burst through Hurt's abdomen, jumped up on the platform, and commenced singing "hello my ragtime gal" in top hat with cane.

Colbert's Silent Tongue

On January 21, 2013, Colbert's first day as VPOTUS, former Veep Biden reservedly handed over the keys to the Naval Observatory—home to Vice Presidents and their 2nd ladies since 1974. (VPs grumble, however, that the navels are frequently covered up with bulky sweaters, obliging the men to strain their eyeballs and imaginations. Historically, belly balling is a vice Veeps view as vital.)

Colbert showed up bright and early on his first day—after a restful night of inaugural ball hopping.

He swiped his keycard to enter the White House; punched in at the Grand Staircase time-clock; and proceeded to the State Dining Room for his complimentary continental breakfast or, at the very least, a steamy cup of joe. (Colbert had seen "Downton Abbey"; he knew how this worked.)

But, oh my! Delectables and coffee were nowhere to be seen! However, when he spotted the dinner gong, he rubbed his hands happily together. That would do the trick! Just as Colbert was about to strike, he slipped on a stick of butter and hit his head on the bell. The gong was deafening.

Colbert regained consciousness at the White House nurse's office 24-hours later in real time. He awoke his usual irreverent self, but when he opened his mouth to ask what ridiculous trauma transpired, he was overcome with a fear of public speaking. Colbert choked on his words. He needed the Heimlich to even force out a "hello"!

President Stewart arrived for the nurse's report, which described Colbert's vernacularly catatonic condition. Stewart gasped, remembering that the VP's commencement speech at WA's Walla Walla College's D.C. Extension was within the hour!

Stewart consulted with strategic advisors **Donald O'Connor** and **Gene Kelly**, and the three came up with a brilliant idea:

1.) Stewart hires a charismatic male speaker.
2.) Colbert stands on stage at Walla Walla and lip-synchs his script.
3.) The charismatic man behind the curtain delivers the speech.

Stewart made a call, and, faster than the speed of frightening, **Bill O'Reilly** was at the door—ready for rehearsal.

The curtain stunt worked so seamlessly that Stewart contracted O'Reilly to do Colbert voiceovers at *all* VP speaking events.

Funny thing is, it turns out Colbert and O'Reilly were *already* working this scheme for "The Colbert Report." Really the only people who know Colbert's true voice are his wife, kids, and whoever watched Colbert's first feature film "Let it Snow" (1999).

Stewart's Cabinet Unhinged

Choosing the right cabinet is a challenge we all deal with: be it our starter house, our timeshare, or our first presidency. Fortunately, White Home Depot is there to help—with a diverse array of in-stock and custom-made choices. The first step, White Home Depot says, is to ask yourself: What kind of Cabinet can I sleep with and what will my Budget allow?

SOS!
To start, Stewart selected Conan O'Brien as his Secretary of State. Stewart deemed O'Brien "a stand up gentleman—civilized and well-red."

The comedians had made amends after their infamous "I Heart Applebees" feud in '08 in which (under Colbert's watchful guard) they fisticuffed over which one of them could eat the most backbone.

O'Brien was also in need of a boost to which Stewart was sympathetic. (O'Brien's wife, Elizabeth, had deserted their marriage and kids to serve as make-out artist for Powell on "American Idol"—leaving O'Brien in the trying role of solo dad.)

An ecstatic O'Brien got the big news just as he was cementing his footprint in the Hollywood Walk of Fame. In jubilation, he raced across the country by foot (weighted down with residual cement) to accept the post—camera crew at his side.

He reached D.C. in under an hour, but, unfortunately, O'Brien only lasted seven months as SOS—likely due to the physical toll of running across the country with blocks of cement on his feet.

O'Brien was so exhausted he could only perform his job functions remotely via Skype on his Lenovo.

Stewart looked the other way as long as he could, but his neck couldn't take it any longer when Internet censorship in Uzbekistan interfered with O'Brien's diplomatic dinner with President **Islam Karimov**.

With O'Brien off the screen, Stewart scrambled to find a new SOS. He considered enlisting buoyant personalities **Al Gore** or **John Kerry**.

But Gore was finishing the last sketch of his run in a Cheatham County Community Theater production of "The Ice Man Commeth," and Kerry, to the nation's astonishment, was leaving politics to open a "My Little Pony®" gift shop at the Fresh Pond Mall in Cambridge.

In desperation, Stewart placed a "Help Wanted" ad in the *Village Voice* classifieds which listed the job requirements. In 2012 *Village Voice* classifieds ran $70 for 40 words. Due to budgetary cuts, Stewart trimmed the ad down to 15 words for $50— eliminating the phone screen and the prerequisite the secretary type 65 words a minute.

The vacancy was eventually filled out by **Dolly Parton**, whose only demand was to work a 9-to-5 (Eastern) schedule.

Second Class Secretaries
Having secured Parton in his grip, Stewart appointed the following non-perishables to his cabinet:

Press Secretary—**Dear Abby**
Secretary of the Interior—**Elle Décor**
Secretary of Transportation—**Miss Daisy**
Secretary of Energy—**Dietrich Mateschitz** (Founder of Red Bull GmbH)
Secretary of Defense—**Fred Gailey** (Santa Claus's defense attorney in 1947's "Miracle on 34th Street")
Secretary of the Treasury—**Captain Jack Sparrow**
Secretary of Veteran Affairs—**John McCain**
Secretary of Housing and Urban Development—**Eminem** (Chocolate manufacturer, not to be confused with wrapper)
Attorney General—**The Marlboro Man**

Secretary of Agriculture:
Stewart struggled with filling this fertile post. His first choice: Greek mythology's **Demeter**, Goddess of Agriculture. But Demeter was only available six months of the year (citing family matters).

Disheartened by the whole "temperamental goddess" thing, Stewart considered inviting **John Franklin** (child actor in 1984's "Children of the Corn") to step into the row. (The Administration wouldn't question Franklin about his questionable background check—given his character Isaac was a minor at the time of the event in question.)

Finally, Stewart fixed himself on enclosing an earthly woman: He presented SOA to **Andrew Wyeth's Christina,** who rose to the occasion to accept the position.

(For a full list of Stewart's secretaries, see calluspas.com.)

Samantha's Bees and John's Olives

President Stewart—with the futile help of Shepherd's Woodworks, Inc. in Lubbock—had difficulty recruiting and retaining a staff of solid support.

After a 37-minute wait in line, Stewart succeeded in getting Best Bed and Beyond's® Geek Squad to extend their reach to headhunting via their pillow division.

The Geek Squad attempted to woo Stewart's former "Daily Show" cohort **Samantha Bee** as Sting Operations Manager. (Responsibilities included spying under covers at the Scripps National Spelling Bee to catch cheaters.)

But Bee was stuck on becoming an astronaut—filling the spacesuit of **Buzz Aldrin** and *ful*filling his mission to discover a Bit O'Honey® in Mars®.

The Geek Squad approached another "Daily Show" newscaster: **John Oliver**. Oliver cheerfully accepted the grim position of International Director of the Division of Family, Child Services and Transportation (DFCST).

Sadly, Oliver's first assignment became his last.

Stewart had assigned Oliver the diplomatic task of trying to sway **Vladimir Putin's** mind about the (then) recently-passed Russian legislation which prohibits Americans from adopting Russian children and highways.

On behalf of an anonymous American couple who had adopted a much-needed highway in Kamchatka—only to have the deal null and void!—Oliver flew to Kamchatka (which cannot be reached by road). His mission: To pave the way to an agreement with the Russians to bring the highway back to its documented U.S. home.

Oliver, when in Rome (FCO transfer to PKC) caught wind of a Moscowian child abuse scandal involving corporal punishment at the Kremlin's military orphanage. Oliver made a surprise guest appearance at the orphanage (PKC to DME) to politely interrogate the manager about the facility's childrearing practices.

Oliver's Russian translation of "Please Sir, I want some more (information)" came out as "Никогда не позвольте мне уезжать, даже если я спрашиваю к."

Loosely translated in English, this means "Never let me leave even if I ask to." To this day, the Kremlin's orphanage is holding Oliver without release. He is under the strict watch of **Miss Hannigan**, who orders him to spear toothpicks with olives for her bathwater gin martinis.

The Incorporation of Congress and the Inferiority Complex of the SEC

During the Stewart presidency, the nation underwent a dramatic restructuring of its political body: the merger of the U.S. Senate and the U.S. House of Representatives.

Since 1789, the two entities had operated as independent subsidiaries of their umbrella company, Congress. In 2014, the C-levels of Congress made the "executive" decision to merge the subsidiaries into one corporation. (Its business entity title: "Incorporated Congress of the United States.")

The corporation went public on the New York Stock Exchange in the summer of '15 under the ticker ICUS and shares have since shot though the dome. ICUS is also traded on the London and Paris stock exchanges under the tickers ICENGLAND, ICFRANCE.

The merger resulted in great strife for—and the ultimate demise of—the ailing Securities Exchange of Currency (and Baseball Cards) (SEC(BC)).

The SEC(BC) was ill-prepared for the influx of insider trading. Nor were they prepared for **Gordon Gekko's** return in the "Occupy Wall Street" sequel.

The SEC(BC) suffered total meltdown. They stopped cashing checks, exchanging currency, giving loans on payday, and issuing vehicle stickers. Feeling vulnerable, the chairmen regrouped to form the Insecurities Exchange Commission (IEC).

Today, the IEC has two functions: 1.) to service self- complex sufferers without self-sufficient support, and 2.) to handle a hotline for struggling salesmen who work on commission.

Baseball cards were left entirely out of the equation.

Part II

ROMANTIC ESCAPADES AND THE NSA

The Sexting Scandal of Petraeus and Paula

During Stewart's term there were scandals galore—the most titillating involved former CIA (Conspicuous Infidelity Agency director **David Petraeus**. While in his post, Petraeus (a married man) would ritually rollerblade with his biographer **Paula Abdul** in Afghanistan.

However, their Yahoo! greeting e-card exchanges were leaked—the content bursting with innuendos. So the NSA (Not So Anonymous) began monitoring Petraeus's and Abdul's texting data.

The first confiscated text was a message to Petraeus from Abdul that read "I8U." The NSA misinterpreted the "8,"—thinking Abdul meant "I hate you."

But NSA director **John C. Linglis's** teenage son poked his head into the matter to explain the text's meaning was "I ate you." This intimation Linglis found quite cunning, and an even *greater* threat which clearly involved cannibalism.

However, Petraeus's texted reply to Abdul read "U can 8 me, if I can 8 U."

The NSA smelled something fishy, and—assuming something was up—thenceforth collected all of the twosome's texts—which NSA's computer lab technician decoded.

Text Transcript Petraeus/Abdul – Exchanged Spring 2012

ABDUL: **SHH (69)**
Secret Meeting

PETRAEUS: **UR ^ MYN ^?**
Your place or mine?

ABDUL: **HM-BN@UR^**
Never been to yours

PETRAEUS: **I :0! IF U :0!**
I'll show you mine if you show me yours

ABDUL: **U #&*(@ ---> .... ;)**
You are a naughty soldier...I like it

PETRAEUS: **MY--'>***U**
My pistol is cocked for you

ABDUL: **BAM et al – WEE...**
All guns and no play...

PETRAEUS: *****POW**
Shoot

ABDUL: **I?\UR $**
I thought that was your job

PETRAEUS: **N! IM ****POW 8^... :(**
No, I mean shoot, wife's here...sorry

ABDUL: **K _ (US)**
OK, keep us under cover

PETRAEUS: **BYOB?**
See you at the mosque tomorrow night?

ABDUL: **I@BOO! U/M ( ) ."[{}]" oo!**
I'll wear a mask! We'll have our own little "mosquerade" ball!

PETRAEUS: **LOL(IYH)**
Laugh out loud (in your head)

And so, Petraeus resigned from the CIA. Today Petraeus is *Head Counsel of Camp Counselors* of the Boy Scouts of America, and steers the Bring the Scouts to the Middle East (BSME) initiative.

E-Dating Hackers Spread Virus

STDs went viral in the fall of '14 when online dating websites were hacked by the outfit Virtual Afflictions Group (VAG). It turns out the VAG masterminds had been devising this hack-job for over a decade. There were early signs of suspicious activity—dating back to the late nineties upon the founding of Match.com.

In 2003, the FBHI (Federal Bureau of Hacker Investigations) supplied (then) President **George W. Bush** with Intelligence that agents had discovered a deserted makeshift computer lab with suspicious vials of viruses. The FBHI reported signs of "weapons of Match destruction" to the president. Bush, however, was incapable of processing the Intelligence, and led the nation to war.

The virus was catastrophic to the single and the married-guys-pretending-to-be-single (MGPTBS) communities.

The STD ("Singles to Destruction") virus worked like this: whenever the dating website user sent an electronic "wink" to another user, that wink carried a Hermes virus that delivered messages between the Clods and Portals. The messages contained traces of Mercury—transmitting toxic chemicals. Circuits crisscrossed and mass infected major cities. Then the circuits came to towns.

Soon all the users' profiles experienced "pins and needles sensations" ("Mercury Poisoning," *Cases Journal, 2009*) and lost their electronic libido. One user reported that—since his online profile got infected with Mercury—"after having sex I feel very run down and some of my symtoms [symptoms] get a little worst [worse]" ("Sex and Mercury Poisoning," *anonymous, Orbis Vitare Forum.com*).

Disillusioned with dating websites, singles and MGPTBS blew up their online accounts with F-bombs, and turned to *It's Just Punch* ® to fill their voids.

At *It's Just Punch* (a face-to-face dating service), matchmakers set up innocent luncheons for love-starved professionals. Thanks to *It's Just Punch*, singles and MGPTBS could meet without the sexual awkwardness that alcoholic drinks at bars inevitably provoke: "Oooh, she thinks I'm witty!" "Will he ever shut up?" "Oooh, I think she's going to let me kiss her!" "Eewww, his lips look like skinned seals."

VAG, however, reconstructed to form PNIS (Party of No Interest in Sobriety).

The Party concocted a chemical formula CH_3CH_2OH to spike punch by means of airborne parasites. PNIS injected the parasites with ethanol and a sharpened sweet tooth—attracting the bugs to *hosts serving singles punch*.

In 2016, *It's Just Punch* shuddered due to an influx of bitter sexual harassment lawsuits. The claim: Staggering MGPTBS were subjected to repeated punches by tipsy women, causing serious injury to the men's egos and storylines.

GLOBAL FRICTION AND OTHER TALES OF DISASTERS

The Amazon Plant Invasion

In 2013, man-eating Venus Fly Traps invaded the Amazon jungle. The carnivorous plants grew to gorilla size—getting bigger and bigger with each crunchy insect and small furry mammal they ate.

By 2014 the plants were devouring jaguars and cougars crossing over the hills. But the plants' thirst for blood was still unquenched.

By 2015 they began to threaten the Amazon's human population, which was 188,000 according to the 2010 census. (A 2014 Amazon census was conducted, but the door-to-door census taker and his notebook went unaccounted for.)

Amazons retaliated by wearing "Don't Feed the Plants" t-shirts. When that attire flopped, Amazons inebriated the plants by pouring a great deal of red vine down their traps—in hopes the plants would think it was blood.

But the vine was actually good for the plants' hearts, and they grew *even stronger*.

America stepped in. President Stewart sent naval ships across the ocean to the Amazon, saving 50% on shipping by placing the executive order online. The ship was giftwrapped and labeled "SIRLOIN." The plants clapped their traps together excitedly and pulled the drawstring. Out sprang the U.S. Navy in full combat mode—Trojan Horse style, but in tanks due to the humidity.

The naval combatants slew the plants with tear gas. The traps—and a few innocent bystander willows— wilted in their defeat.

The Amazons expressed their gratitude by granting the strapping sailors tankless gratification with the hot giantess Wonder Woman. The grieving willows were granted tissues for their weepy hollow.

An Infestation of Tics Down Under

A tic infestation in Australia made headlines in 2013.

The cause of the infestation: Australian Aborigines released the tics in rage upon the revelation that **Jeff Fratt**, of "The Wiggles," lied about his aboriginal origins.

Fratt had claimed he was of Aussie Aborigine descent, but was, in fact, an Aborigine from Tahiti.

You see, Fratt had been pulled over by authorities (for sleeping at the wheel of his big red car) on Wanneroo Road. They popped the trunk only to find Fratt's Tahitian passport alongside some monoi oil and noni.

The tics spread throughout the Australian continent—which some argue is not one. Now all Australians are nervously shrugging their shoulders in jerky, choppy motions. Australians heed the UN (United Neuroses) annually at general assemblies—imploring the UN to mandate international research to identify a cure.

But the UN clearly doesn't take them seriously. The diplomats from down under keep shrugging jerkily—so it's generally assumed the Aussies are indifferent to their own entreaty.

Australian scientists have tried to invent a cure *themselves*, but their incessant shrugging causes them to drop their beakers, spilling chemicals onto their sneakers—hence not getting anywhere unscathed.

Empathetic to the hassle of tics down under, President Stewart has assured Australian Prime Minister **Elvis Abbot** that he will meet with him personally (where Elvis lives) to ponder potential presidential preferential treatments in May. (In May DCA/SYD flights are the most economical on Expedia and CheapTics.com.)

McDonalds Serves Freedom Flies

In May 2012, U.S./France relations hit a cul de sac when the French people elected **François Hollande** as their President.

Hollande's allegiance to the Socialist Party stirred—what came to be known as—"The Mold War." McDonalds Corporation took patriotic action by changing the name of their "French Fries" to "Freedom Fries."

However, McDonalds' copywriter committed a grave typo on the new menus. When typing "Fries," she accidentally hit the "L" key instead of the "R." Over 14,000 McDonalds' restaurants advertised they served "Freedom Flies."

To make matters worse, the same copywriter committed *another* typo by adding an "S" to "OIL." McDonalds' new menus boasted they fried their flies in "Vegetable Soil."

(The copywriter also accidentally omitted salads from the menu, but was relieved when no one noticed.)

As a result, the Department of Shelf and Cumin Services (DOSACS)—charged with the inspection of infested facilities, moldy sauce and spices—intervened.

DOSACS inspectors inspected the menu, and concluded "yes," the fast food was beset with insects and mold. DOSACS prohibited McDonalds from selling fries and placed an order to replace McDonalds' vegetable oil with Hollandaise sauce.

Consequently, McDonalds suffered a financial wallop, and as a cost-cutting measure, stopped stuffing toys in Happy Meals.

But The Mold War ended in 2014 when **Gérard Depardieu** made a big appearance in the film "Welcome to New York." McDonalds regained market share by offering its gourmet "Joe of Arch" coffee, "McSalad Niçoise," and "McFoie Gras Burgers."

The Study Abroad Tax Evasion Scandal

For decades the IRS (Inmate Release Service) looked the other way in the face of evasion. But in 2015, the Brain Industry Association (BIA) forced the IRS to collect taxes from clever study-abroad students working as waiters.

The order stemmed from Intelligence that American college students—working under the table— were suffering repeated concussions due to bumping their heads when their shifts were up.

The IRS flew assessors in to assess the situation. The assessors frequented a multitude of eating establishments such as *Hofbräuhaus* in München (Munich); the *Brasserie Julien* in Paris (Paris), *Restaurante Figueira Rubaiyat* in São Paulo (San Paulo), and 餓的孩子 in 香港 (Hong Kong).

The American students were difficult to locate, but after months of being forced to smell the fat assessors' feet, the students couldn't bear it anymore. They tied the assessors' shoelaces together to trip them up, and escaped from under the tables— bumping their heads on the way.

The Clothing of Guantanamo

In 2015, President Stewart mandated the closing of the Guantanamo Detention Center at the naval base in Cuba. (Stewart was in the 'hood on a musical pursuit of Havana sitars.)

The Administration's intent was to transfer the Guantanamo prisoners to U.S. correctional facilities in Coal County, WV in order to expand their mines.

One prisoner put up a major fuss: **Robert Opel**. Opel was imprisoned for streaking at the 46th Academy Awards ceremony in 1974 behind actor **David Niven**.

Opel quite fancied the Guantanamo facilities, and had even taken to wearing bed sheet togas. He rallied his fellow inmates to protest the closing by going on an underwear strike and setting themselves on fire by self-flatulation.

The prisoners' efforts were flamefully feeble. In 2016, the U.S. government hired actress-turned-NASA (National Alien Slayer Agency) contractor **Sigourney Weaver** to tackle the shackled. Weaver donned an oxygen helmet and buckled into a mechanical robot suit (courtesy of Caterpillar®) to thwart the naked, unlucky strikers.

Weaver succeeded in stuffing the men back into their jumpsuits. She extinguished their sparks with slime, but not before roasting some Stay Puft Marshmallows® first.

As punishment, a weary, worn-out Opel was sentenced to a weak in solitary consignment.

Italy Loses Color

In fall 2014, a perplexing—but somehow romantic—occurrence occurred in Italy. (To this very day the phenomenon remains unexplained.) We're talking, of course, about when Italy turned black and white.

The first signs—in the summer of '14—were barely noticeable: Italians reported a "La sfumatura dolce grigia nell'aria." (Translation: "slightly grayish hue in the air.") And "Questi giorni il mio accantona sempre Dusty di sguardo." (Translation: "These days my shelves always look dusty.")

But come October, it was as clear as cliché: When people crossed the border into Italy (including Sicily and Sardinia) color vanishes. All of Italy (except San Marino and the Vatican City) is in black and white—and sometimes skips a little, like an old foreign film.

Opponents of the bizarre manifestation were primarily Italian businesspersons serving the tourism industry. The sporadic skipping of Italy—like an old reel of silent film playing—dislodged the Tower of Pisa. The tower toppled atop a tourist shop, dislodging hundreds of miniature ceramic Towers of Pisa off the seemingly-dusty shelves. "What will fall to ruins next!" tour guides complained in vexation, "the Roman Coliseum?!?!"

The Venice Travel Bureau was especially rattled. "Who wants to ride a gondola on canals that look like oil?" the Bureau complained. Today Venetian tourism barely stays afloat; and is at the mere mercy of Turkish, Bulgarian and Romanian tourists—and other vacationers indigenous to the coastal countries along the Black Sea.

Some Italians are actually proponents of the change. For example, old movie buffs and fans of **Federico Fellini's** "8 ½" and "La Dolce Vita"; and the small-minded, who prefer to see things in black and white.

Also, there is disinterest among another group of *Cittadini italiani*. In 2015, Italians who are already colorblind released this statement: "NON RIESCO davvero a vedere che cosa l'affare grande." (Translation: "I really don't see what the big deal is.")

The Controversial Erection of the BOLLYWOOD Sign in Tirumala

To honor Hindi cinema and the old Bombay, the Indian movie-making industry erected a gigantic sign of letters that read "BOLLYWOOD"—modeled after the famous Hollywood sign in California.

The BOLLYWOOD letters were delivered, assembled and up-raised by a collection of children. The chore was filmed documentary-style by British director **Danny Boyle** ("Plum Paw Pill Pun Pear," "Brain-Clotting").

When the BOLLYWOOD sign was erected in 2014—by the all-but-underarm sweat of child labor—the sign's dimensions measured—like its California counterpart—45-ft. tall and 350-ft. long.

The glittering new landmark was strewn with blinking multi-colored Christmas lights and decked with mini-speakers playing Bhangra pop. The BOLLYWOOD sign, oh how it graced the rolling hills of Tirumala!

Upon the release of Boyle's documentary: "A Sign of Good Hill Bunting" (2015), word spread that the children had not been paid for their labor. Humanitarian activists and stage moms—from all parts of the world—flew to Tirumala to protest. They stormed the hill; dismantled the gigantic sign; and hacked it to pieces with machetes and baseball bats. BOLLYWOOD was annihilated.

In the calm after the storm, the Indian movie-making industry negotiated a re-erection of the sign. The entertainment executives agreed to rehire the children and—this time around—pay them with compliments and Boost®.

Part III
DOMESTICATED NUISANCES AND A CRAZY LITTLE THING CALLED WAR

Giving America the New Bird

On August 28, 2013, a bold body of bald men marched on Washington—protesting funding cuts in hair regrowth research.

They stomped atop tens of thousands of 1 dollar bills—to symbolize the government's historical favoritism of bourgeois, bushy-rooted American men—like **George Washington** with his lush white locks.

"My dear folk, please do not hold me accountable: In 1782, America chose the Bald Eagle as its symbol of moral character," President Stewart exclaimed at an emergency press conference. "Therefore, the Bald American People should revel in pride! They should stand tall, beaming in their shine. Alas, today's march affirms that bald Americans do not take this stance."

The press conference's court reporter, **Brenda Starr,** pointed out: "Perhaps the protesters are offended by the Bald Eagle's imminent extinction,"—typing her words as she spoke.

The president proclaimed that perfectly plausible, and—to appease the men's furry—Stewart appointed a new national bird: The African Grey Parrot.

This sophisticated feathered friend has been called the "perfect mix of brains and beauty" (*Bird Talk*, Aug. '92) and the "Cadillac of parrots" (*Bird Talk*, Sept. '93).

Stewart received wide-spread support. After all, the Cadillac was an American car—a division of the Ford Motor Company. The rechristening was fowlproof!

And so the African Grey Parrot became the new emblem of American patriotism: A symbol of a changing demographic with a charming sense of parrody.

The Fraggles' Fuss about Fracking

In '15, the famous fracking site of Fellsmere, Fl. furnished a flabbergasting finding, not unlike the fossils found in Pompeii, Pa.

The hydraulic-fracking miners injected the flammable fluid into the site's squeaky floorboards and inserted a vacuum through the crack to suck up fossil fuel. To the miners' amazement, the nozzle guzzled the *fossil* but not the fuel.

What the miners retrieved from the rock was, in fact, the remains of **Boober Fraggle**—the beloved puppet from **Jim Henson's** "Fraggle Rock" (1983-1987).

The dead Fraggle's encrusted arms were extended—one stuck mid-wave. Poor Boober no longer resembled his early self: blue-green complexion, orange mop of hair, animated essence—gone without a trace.

No, Boober's felt was soaked with soot, his hair wriggled with worms, his eyes popped out of their sockpuppets. (Given that Boober Fraggle never had eyes to begin with, forensics confirmed the puppet's identity without subjecting the furry corpse to frenetic testing.)

The finding of the exhumed Fraggle ignited outrage among Former Fraggle Followers (FFF). Chants of "Fracking is a folly!"; "Don't frack until you're ready!"; "Burial for Boober!" and "We're not your puppets!" filled the air in Washington.

In an attempt to appease the mob, President Stewart alerted FFF to the fact that he *himself* was a Jim Henson fan—citing **Miss Piggy's** guest appearance on "The Daily Show" in 1999 and his own debut on "Sesame Street" (2007, Episode 4,156).

Fraggle purists were not pacified. They argued that—despite design by the same maker—Muppets were a different breed.

But FFF eased off when Stewart granted Boober a proper burial—no strings attached. The funeral procession was aired live on HBO and CBC (Canada). The scene was somber and poignant—an American flag draped over the casket case in which Boober lay.

The Mississippi Missile Crisis

No American will forget the Mississippi Missile Crisis in October 2013. It began when a naval officer and a gentlewoman met on the Biloxi wharf.

The officer picked up on her classy airs, and—for a pick-me-up—invited her to biscuits and tea as a pickup. During their herbal tryst, the officer received a call on his walkie talkie from his commanders.

Knowing it's improper to take a call during tea, the officer whispered into his walkie: "Can't talk. Time for lunch. Holding hot bread. Biloxi bomb shell. Sweater tight. Nude-colored slacks. Wow. I'll ask if she's got a sister. (Murmur.) She don't. Will be late tomorrow morning at the ship. Yowza!!!"

The static clinging to the line caused the commanders to hear: "Can't talk. Time for launch. Holding me hostage. Biloxi bombs and shells. Better fight. Nuclear attack. Ow. I'll ask if they'll stop the missile. (Murmur.) They won't. Kill at 8 tomorrow morning or I'm whipped. Ouch, ahhh!!!"

When President Stewart caught wind of the Mississippi missiles, he commanded the <u>Defensive Ministry of Violence</u> (DMV) to reposition its nuclear telescope 1,276 km NW to target Biloxi.

The president ordered a warning missile fired to show Mississippi that the U.S. meant business.

The missile penetrated an abandoned bomb shelter built by visionaries during the Civil War. Barrels of baked beans exploded—spraying airborne debris across all of Harrison County.

Mississippians cheered, fetched their banjoes, and circled 'round the campfire—roasting weenies and shooting the breeze. It took 13 days to clean up the mess.

After FEMA had rung out its massive mop, Mississippi was deemed safe, and DMV's nuclear telescope repositioned itself sturdily back to Aruba.

A Crockpot of Bull and the Texas Secession

Since 1885 Texas had been dying to secede from the Union. Secession petitions are reviewed by the president only when the petitioning entity produces a minimum of 25,000 signatures in one day.

(This requirement was put in place by 1st POTUS, George Washington—persuaded by his bff **John Hancock** to sign the policy into effect. In 1910, President **William Taft** added an appendix to the law that permitted electronic signatures and "Likes" as valid tallies.

Some speculate Taft was sucking up to **Thomas Edison** who owned the Edison's Electronic Write Company and invented the sociable media platform for the telegraph. Others say Taft added the appendix as a cautionary measure should he lose his.)

booksonawhim.com

On December 29, 2015, the State of Texas's Facebook "Petition for an Independent Texas" page received the 25,000 "Likes" it needed to be acknowledged by President Stewart.

The State was startled by just how quickly Stewart acquiesced to their plea. On December 30, 2015, President Stewart awoke to circumcise Texas from the U.S. just after showering.

Boy, was *that* a painful operation! Before **Melissa and Doug**® could redesign their "Deluxe Wooden USA Map Puzzle"®, many technicalities had to be pieced together. Namely, San Antonio and Austin.

The two cities were in a tizzy about "this whole secession thing." Their combined 2,225,543 (and one-on-the-way) population did not *want* to be snipped off from their mother country.

President Stewart presented two options:

1. San Antonions and Austonions could give the new Republic of Texas a shot—like the remaining 23,833,660 (and one-on-the-way-out) of the gun-slaphappy Texans—and embrace their puns and clay pigeons.

2. Texans could build a 49-ft. wall around both cities. San Antonio and Austin would be designated U.S. Commonwealths—granted the right to vote in U.S. elections. The stipulation: Texas's 38 electoral votes would be divided equally between the liberal Commonwealths.

In the end, San Antonio opted to relinquish their U.S. citizenship, and Austin opted for the wall. Requirements included:

1. "The Austin City Limits" radio show had to be brought within city limits.

2. San Antonio could keep Waxy O'Connor's Irish Pub on the Riverwalk, but the Alamo had to go. Its Texas ties were just too trite. Plus it was a landmark of a famous piece of U.S. history: **Davy Crocker's** patriotic mechanical bull showdown against **Al Capone**. (Crocker later married baker **Betty**, an American icon in her own bite.)

On February 14, 2016—around breakfast time—the U.S. airlifted the Alamo to Birmingham, Alabamo. But after doing so, the U.S. realized they really didn't know what to do with the darn thing. Americans were disappointed. It was much smaller than it looked in the postcards.

So—around dinner time—the Alamo was airlifted to Las Vegas, Nevada where it now resides without complaint between the long legs of the Eiffel Tower.

The Perfume Wars

Speaking of Marseille, what came to be called "The Perfume Wars" was a snotty battle begun in Switzerland.

"The Perfume Wars," of course, is the appellation Americans put upon themselves to pervade. The French Suisse, French Canadiens and French Côte d'Ivoirians told the Americans (in French) to put a lid on it—dubbing the combat "la guerre d'eau de toilette."

"The Perfume Wars" was a 3-year contest of indigenous noses that took face in June 2015. From Bogotá, Columbia where the South American winds blow; to Mokolodi, Botswana where the rhinos roam: All countries were game.

Top contenders were Switzerland's "Eau de Fromage"—concocted in the Gruyères, and the U.S.A.'s "Eau de Tuna"—created in Albacoreque, New Mexico.

To everyone's surprise, an underdog won the war: China's "Eau de la Foot," whose inventor said he knew his product was bound to win.

HEALTH AND EPIDEMICS

The Whore on Drugs

In the early 1900s, **Bertha Palmer**—wealthy socialite for whom Chicago's swanky Palmer House was built—invented the brownie by means of her chef. (He had money too.) Palmer was an esteemed, elegant woman.

But Palmer's reputation plummeted when—in 1905—word broke that she had posed for **Auguste Rodin**, sculptor of erotic poses. (Rodin's most controversial works: "The Eskimo Genital Kiss," "The Humping Dogs," and "The Bust of Bertie.")

Although it wasn't given a head, "The Bust of Bertie" was voyeuristically reviewed as vulgar. The public figured out Bertha was the model the day she hid her head in shame when she guessed the public was about to figure her out.

Sensing Palmer's susceptibility, a jealous **Camille Claudel**—resentful that her lover Rodin didn't let *her* sculpt Palmer's bust—stirred cannabis into Palmer's Chamomile. Weak with rue, Palmer succumbed to infusions.

Within a week, she was sprinkling cannabis on her crabs. Within a month, the dame was mixing marijuana into her brownies with the help of her chef. (He had attendants too.)

By 1907, Palmer was so strung out she fled to Mexico City via Nevada in her Tin Lizzie. She was *hungry*. She *needed bread*. Having thrown away her fortune—she drove about in fear and loafing for lost wages.

In Mexico City, fed up with food stamps that sullied her tongue, Palmer founded an institute of higher earning: a weed-garden bakery—christened "Potter's Panadería de Hierbajo." (She assumed her husband's forename **"Potter"** because it was just too perfect.)

But in 1910 Mexican authorities arrested Palmer for potsitution.

Ninety-eight years later, POTUS Stewart called on Americans to pay respects to the founding mother of the brownie. Stewart, who appeared in the film "Half Baked" (1998), sympathized with the plight of the woman baker.

(At first Americans were doobieous about their duty. But after a few deep breaths, they paid their tokings of respect.)

Palmer lived out her remaining years cramped in a cell in Cerro de los Guerreros (Warrior's Hill). Empathetically, Stewart drafted an extension of the medical use of marijuana to women suffering PMS—a measure spotted to take effect in 2018 on the 100th anniversary of Palmer's death.

The Regeneration of the Smartphone into the Human Hand

The first Smartphone "**Simon**" was introduced in 1992 by IBM (I Borrow Money). Twenty-three years later (2015), 91% of adult Americans have at least 1 Smartphone and 1 child named Simon. Now (2016), the average household has more Smartphones than smart people.

By 2010, Smartphones had become a fixture in human hands. By 2014, "users" became "abusers." By 2015, "abusers" became "addicts."

Human hands that possessively clutched Smartphones—during sleep, herding sheep, etc.—evolved. Addicts' metacarpal anatomy began to mimic their owner's perpetual grip.

Hands transformed—curling as if cupping crests, thumbs aslope. Addicts were unfazed. In fact, their deformed hands made texting and emailing *easier*.

Soon Smartphones started sticking to the flesh of palms and no longer needed charging. The devices mutated into living leech-like organisms—sucking static energy out of the addicts' skin cells to thrive.

Fingers fused into touchscreens. Knuckles kneaded into networks. Addicts could no longer pick up a fork without it dropping to the floor. How could they eat if they always knew someone was coming? Even worse, they *couldn't dial or type* without fingers! High fives hurt, and playing a game of "rock paper scissors" was just about impossible.

SAMHSA (Smartphone Abuse and Metal Hand Services Administration) drew a parallel and made a parable about the afflicted and **Tantalus**.

Tantalus—a ravenous Greek God—was tortured in wrath by grapes dangling before him. The juicy fruit was almost…but not quite…in reach.

SAMHSA went on to compare the afflicted to **Little Bunny Foo Foo**. Like Tantalus, Foo Foo was tortured by food dangling before him. In Foo Foo's case, it was carrots, not grapes. The carrots were a mere hop, skip, and a jump away…But Foo Foo was rooted in place, and could only follow the carrots with his eyes.

The worst cases (people who stare at their Smartphones while jaywalking, driving in farm-worker zones, nursing newborns, etc.) suffered "neck freeze." This is when the addict's neck stiffens while looking down—glazed eyes gazing at their screen.

Their eyes function like gravitationally-sucked suction cups and *stick* to the screen—eyelids raised, eyes agape. The addict's cellular hands stick like superglue to his or her eyeballs—surfing in an un-blink-away-able glare.

The <u>Fire Department Administration</u> (FDA) tried to unstick the addicts' eyeballs from their screens by employing the frozen-tongue-stuck-to-the-pole treatment method. But pouring hot water into the victims' eyes only steamed their screens.

Addicts steamed: How could they surf the web in water?!

Some addicts actually embraced their mutation. For example, cutting edge lovers had QR codes tattooed to their bodies so they could feel each other up.

In February 2016—just as addicts were finally getting a grip on their deformities—**Daniel Day Lewis** appeared in the new film "My Left Hand," portraying an afflicted Smartphone addict.

Lewis's performance was so *brilliant*...so *poignant*...there wasn't a dry eye in the house. The movie-goers' buttery and salty tears short-circuited their cellular hands, which subsequently exploded.

Shell-shocked addicts exited the cinema squinting—as if seeing the light of day for the very first time.

The healing addicts' human hands sprouted back—though forever slightly incurvated, cupping the air in withdrawal.

The Long Term Effects of Lasik Come to Light

In 2014, an unsightly scare scared scared Americans scared about the scare:

On May 13 the nation—poised to ring in the 64th birthday of **Stevie Wonder**—witnessed a wondrous sight. Like any other May 13 sunset (8:14 pm D.C. time), the moon shone on the U.S.—but this eve its rays ricocheted off landlocked American borders. The moonshine staggered into Canadian and Mexican checkpoints, got turned away, and spun.

In awe, the people beamed at the beams spinning and bouncing across this Land. (The Americans' diverted attention irked Wonder, who had always felt overshadowed by **Rays.)**

The next day, 8 million Americans awoke to an alarming spectacle: The white part of their eyes (scar-era) had turned into stained glass!

16 million scareras were now mosaic-patterned—sprinkled with sensational shapes and shiny shades of color.

Because their pupils were unaffected, the *people* affected could still see. However, most propped their eyelids up with toothpicks or cotton swabs in fear that blinking would shatter the glass and pierce their sight.

After a deep investigation conducted by Visual Spyes®, the public learned that stained glass scarera was a Lasik surgery- related reaction. Something about the moon's rays that May evening—cast upon Americans who used to lose and bump into things—turned cracked eye-whites into stained glass.

American Lasik under-goners—with the exception of ASASSSS (<u>American Society of Apathetics, Self-Suppressors and Self- Sadists</u>) members—rallied (having found new vigor) at the White House.

Their reproach: America MUST find a cure or, at the very least, a Band-Aid approach that sticks. Millions shouted in unison, "I scream, you scream, we all scream for eye cream!"—over and over.

Their voices got louder and louder. First soprano **Maria Aloysia Antonia Weber** chimed in with the same G6 she trilled in "Popoli di Tessaglia"—a concerto **Wolfgang Amadeus Mozart** wrote especially for her.

The G6 was *so high* it shattered the stained glass in all 8 million Lasiked-Americans. Mosaic shards showered to their feet.

Victims screamed bloody murmur—until they saw their vision was still intact, their scareras again were white!

Why, the mosaic had *not* been glass, but was rather harmless ceramic pieces of dried clay—crusty hardened residue that need only break to expose healthy, 20/20 eyes.

Ophthalmologists resumed performing Lasik procedures, and pottery artists were staffed in the surgery rooms to save the clay.

AN ECONOMIC COLLAPSE AND ITS NIPPLE EFFECT

The Rise and Fall of the White Bread Factory: Cutting off the Trust

In Dec. 2007, Americans lost their grip when a recession pushed the country into a downward slide rail.

The recession was sparked by the collapse of Wells Fargo when Fargo kept falling down because it had too far to go. So Wells branched off to start the <u>Wells Endowedment for the Arts</u>. (Opening ceremony featured **Paul T. Anderson's** "Boogie Nights" on ride screen.)

All across the U.S. of A., hardworking slackers and slacking hard workers lost their jobs. Hundreds of thousands of people lost their livelihoods—due to mass layoffs by corporations such as Specific Motors (107,357), Ruralgroup (73,056), Merrill- Hug (40,650), and JP Morgan...Run! (22,852). Big box stores folded or went corrugated—sending ripples of disorder across America.

The hardest hit were the white bread workers in Wheaton, IL.

The White Bread Factory, "Flavor Less Dough: Crust as You Like It®," in Wheaton was known for its—light, simple and practical—all-American product.

In its heyday (November 30, 2007), Flavor Less Dough employed roughly 9,177,877 white bread workers in the State of Illinois. When the recession rained in (December 1, 2007), consumers stopped bringing home *any* kind of bread—even soggy. The bread makers were made rebundant and the factory closed.

At first the euphemistically-coined "bite-sized" rolled with it, but they soon realized man can only live by bread alone. It didn't matter how you sliced it; without bread, they were not men.

Melba Lara of *WBEZ-Chicago* interviewed the bread worker emeriti. Their plea to the president: "Bail us out of this cr*p!" (rhymes with sap). Lara's microphone blew a fuse, an Americans who were paying attention heard: "Bail us out of this crop!" (rhymes with mop).

(Then) President Obama wasn't sure how to respond. So he decided to play it by ear—emptying out a bale of corn on a vacant lot. The laid-off bread makers assembled in a line, and waited their turn for their ration.

Obama-Éclair (The Affordable Heath-Bar Act) and the Smithsonian Sweet Tooth

On June 28, 2012, the U.S. Supreme Court held up a federal statue sculpted by (then) President Obama out of hard dark chocolate. The statue had been a monument of contention between liberals and conservatives since Obama carved it into law on March 23, 2010.

The law was technically titled "The Affordable Heath-Bar Act," but was nicknamed "Obama-Éclair" by the common man.

The law obliged every U.S. business owner—with more than 49 personnel—to indulge each employee with complimentary chocolate bars and pastries. Owners who neglect to comp pie were to be assigned the toilsome task of injecting jelly into donuts and braiding lattice on pie tops.

Obama-Éclair also required Americans to buy chocolate bars and pastries for themselves and their families—thus ensuring adequate coverage for unexpected house calls and sleepovers.

The law included a mandate that bulky Americans receive portions equal to those procured by the flimsy. "No body will be denied chocolate due to its weight!" Obama sang out.

Republicans were teething they were seething so much! They tried to rally dentist opposition to the Act® with Temptations But dentists didn't bite. (In fact, dentists forecasted the act reeling in some real revenue in fillings!)

However, Republicans did win over *one* dentist-turned-public servant. Supreme Court Justice **Diana Floss** voted against Obama-Éclair. But Floss's vote was purely a symbolic gesture in a jealous stage against (60s girl group) **Candy and the Kisses.**

[In '81, Floss became the first woman justice appointed to the judicial branch. Before her appointment, the Supreme Court justices were suing the federal government to change their institution's appellation to: Steamy Court Racquetball of the United Men (SCROTUM). By the time their case made it to the Supreme Court, Floss had attained her seat. All it took was a little basic instinct and a leg lift "chair stare": Floss got all the balls in her court and the branch's name stayed set in stone.]

Three Years in the Running

Obama-Éclair launched October 1, 2013. It's been a rocky road, but today the act is widely savored.

Business owners, in fact, quite *like* inducing chocolate lethargy in their employees. Trends demonstrate that today's employees fill up on free sweets and forgo lunch breaks—increasing their productivity due to sugar highs.

And senior citizens are pleased that Medaéclaire provides them the plummest pickings in pastries at a reduced gait—and the unpopular Part D coverage gap (known as the "donut hole") will be closed by 2020.

Form and Sustenance

As a result of the highly flavorable Obama-Éclair, the human body evolved "Survival of the Unfittest" style. Women got loose and hippier. Men grew fleshy breasts—this enlarged their (now pancake-sized) nipples.

Culture and technology evolved: "Social Media" switched into "Ice Cream Socials." The Internet inserted candy stripers into their URLs. Starbucks® swapped coffee with hot melted toffee. And… when Obama-Éclair mandated the lollypop replace the drumstick, Chick Filet® changed its name to Lick Filet® in expectation the peppermint would replace the patty.

A Moveable Sweet

Science and art metamorphosed with the rollout of Obama-Éclair. The Smithsonian was the first host of such realms to adapt.

In the spring of 2015, the Smithsonian trumpeted its new revolutionary exhibit: "A Moveable Sweet."

The tasteful exhibit—rumored to soon be made permanent—showcases a gallery of confections made ambulatory by demand.

The apex of the exhibit is the *live demonstration of confectionary evolution*. Smithsonian scientists:
1. Slice gummy worms in half—both halves keep moving; and
2. Chop the heads off chocolate chickens—whose headless bodies run about in panic madly.

PART IV

THE PRESIDENTS PLAYHOUSE

The White House is a Fun House: From Remote Control Drones to "Being John Edwards"

After swearing into office, President Stewart married into a worldly country of astronomical debt. Economists attribute the nation's debt to two humiliating box office bombs:

1.) Democrats' poorly-made investment in the short-lived "Yes, We Can!" musical revue on ice.
2.) Republicans' poorly-made investment in the Fox Sci-Fi animated series: "Star Wars 84: Missile Defense Gone Ballistic."

With a deficit of more dollars than China has puppies (wagging and stewed), Stewart's political advisor **Axl Rose** advised drastic measures must be mistaken.

Stewart retired to the Oval Office, put his feet up on his desk, and reclined back in his swivel chair. He placed his hands behind his head, and an arresting idea cuffed him:

"I will turn the White House into a Fun House!!! We'll demand a buck a head...or some doe if we charge the ladies. The Fun House's profits will pay off America's debt and accept charge cards so Americans can sink deeper into it!"

White House renovations went underway immediately, and the Fun House debuted in April 2015.

Stewart established a senior committee to manage the Operation with tweezers. The committee went by the acronym "PAYTOPLAY" which stood for "Patriotic Americans Yearn To Operate Play-doh, Legos, And Yahtzee."

PAYTOPLAY stripped the lobby floors, replacing the marble with gymnastic mats. The committee painted the White House exterior with a fresh coat of bright white paint, and stuck glow-in-the-dark sticker stars on the interior ceilings for slumber parties.

In "The East Room," space was cleared for the Association of Hypnotists, Exorcists and Motivational-Speakers (AHEM) to provide some phonic relief. For *chronic* relief, "The Situation Room" was reserved for family interventions—citizens and permanent residents only. (At an extra cost, families can rent the Speaker of the House as mediator.)

The Fun House features:
- "Secret Service Segway Hunts" (SSSH)—staged tours to shoot mock assassins
- Mini remote control drones—"no fly zone" games for boys
- Bungee jumping from the debt ceiling
- Donkey and elephant rides
- The Dorian Gray Mirror Maze
- Foodcourt Exotica (seasonal)
- Bouncy castle (by reservation only, checkout's at noon)

President Stewart's brainchild was a prodigy! But not all the rides were propitious…

There was one *calamitous* attraction: the "Being **John Edwards**" ride.

How it worked: Patrons crawled through a duct into a portal to Edwards' brain, and became him for an hour. When the ride was over, the patrons disembarked Edwards' brain feeling filthy and nauseous.

"It's, like, sickening," one pubescent patron was like, "I mean, it's like the President sicced [sic] a dirty jackass on my brain and called it industrious recreation" (SIC code: 7900).

The Stewart Administration shut down the ride—labeling it a mental health hazard.

The Presidents Playhouse: A Cellar Discovery

The Fun House beckoned buses of schoolchildren. Lines of kids littered the walk outside—waiting to be let in.

On June 11, 2015, a 5-year old boy—in a winding, rollicking line—drew the plastic spoon from his cup of sherbet and commenced chipping at the foremost Fun House column. The column crumbled—like dried paper mâché—to reveal a fireman's pole leading underground. The pole was greased, a red stiletto wedged in the tall sheer metal rod.

The pole-leading-underground led to the disclosure of the BIGGEST classified cellar in U.S. history: The Presidents Playhouse.

That *not quite summer* day, the world learned that U.S. presidents have had a secret cellar since the White House was built in 1792. Only they, vice presidents, certain diplomats, select politicians, famous actors, and royal mistresses were granted access—pinky-sworn to secrecy.

Former President **John Adams**—the first president to reside in the new mansion—ordered the cellar built. Adams cited a need for privacy so he could compose the musical masterpiece "Nixon in China."

(Some historians and musicologists theorize that Adams had the cellar built in an effort to feel "geographically closer" to China and to "better capture the Chinese essence" in his work.)

In 1920, the Presidents Playhouse opened a speakeasy: "The Draft Entry." "The Draft Entry" was accessible through a swing door bookshelf in the White House bomb shelter. The speakeasy's tagline: *Once You Enter the Draft, You Never Go Back.*

Other Presidents Playhouse amenities included "**Bill Clinton's** Cigar Bar"; **Spiro Agnew's** "Groovy Disco Dis Bar"; **Joe Biden's** "Biden Yer Time" relaxation spa; **Millard Fillmore's** library for young adult fiction; and the "The Happy and Gay Bipartisan Lounge." The latter featured a unisex restroom with writing on the walls that included "**Harvey Milk** was here (1977)" and "**Barbara Pierce Bush** was here, don't tell Dad (2003)."

Famished presidents and other sweet-toothed VIPs could frequent the CIA's French bakery "Treaties of Verspies," or indulge in a treat from a rusted vending machine—stocked with "The State of Maine Spruce Gum" (1848), "Squirrel Nut Zipper" (1905), "Goo Goo Clusters" (1913), "5th Avenue Candy Bar" (1936), and a "Whistle Pop" (1975).

The Playhouse is enormous. It's been hailed as "a village" and "rec room of the gods." The cellar—insulated with slabs of clay and cobble—has narrow paths and hallways lit with gas streetlamps.

The cellar stretches under pretty much the entire base of the White House. Dignified guests with weary legs could use **FDR's** wheelchair for smooth transit.

And, as there were no ramps when the Playhouse was built, guests could use **Andrew Jackson's** hickory cane to descend *even further*—to reach the secret cellar's wine cellar where Adam's shovel lay to rest.

Now a Fun House highlight (open to the paying public), the Presidents Playhouse showcases dozens of relics and artifacts it accrued during—what has come to be known as—"The Secretive Years" (1792-2015).

Relics include: **JFK's** 45th birthday ice cream cake (sprinkled with frozen spittle); **Richard Nixon's** elongated wooden nose; **Bill Clinton's** elongated wooded sax; **Dan Quayle's** potatoe; **Abraham Lincoln's** applause; **Elvis Presley's** hotness; **Woodrow Wilson's** wife's uncast ballot; **Warren Harding's** poker face on china; **William Taft's** novelty t-shirt "I would gladly pay you Tuesday for a hamburger today"; **Ronald Reagan's** sweet tooth in a jar; the former Hexagon's missing wing; **Pablo Picasso's** *Harlequin Head*; **Andy Warhol's** can opener; **Stanley Kubrick's** *Eyes Wide Shut* chaise lounge; **Grover Cleveland's** bachelor party favors; **Teddy Roosevelt's** "Proud Union Home" yard sign; **Francois Mitterrand's** timeshare; **Michael Ducockpiss's** escape incontinent pet rooster; **Gerald Ford** and **Martin Van Buren's** 2-car garage; **Dennis Haysbert's** trailer; **King George VI's** teleprompter; and Stewart's own contribution: a bar of soap for washed out mouths.

Life after Laughs

Regrettably, the Stewart term is up this year. Pee-Yew Research Center (PYRC) reports a majority of Americans expect Stewart will run for a second term. We can hope, but only Late Night can substantiate the speculation.

Grade A Papers "Cheep Sheet"

CHEEP SHEET

"The Nutty Years of the Jon Stewart Presidency in a Nutshell" paper is laced with whimsicalities:

- random plays on words
- random people—real and unreal
- random spoofs on news, events, gossip and happenings
- random references to movies, books, theater, art and random randomnesses.

This CHEEP SHEET sheds light on this term paper's playful remarks and references.

OBAMA RESIGNS TO HAWAII

Obama Brushes Off Birth Certificate

- "The Amazing Race" is a reality TV show where contestants travel around the world looking for clues that lead them to other destinations—and ultimately $1,000,000.
- "The Apprentice" is a reality TV show led by conservative billionaire Donald Trump. Trump has challenged the authenticity of Obama's birth certificate.

The First Lady Thrusts

- Michelle Obama is known for launching fitness campaigns—especially geared toward youth.
- The Jane Fonda video and thrust movement referred to are real.

A RESURRECTED ELECTION

Republican Primary

- In the 1990 TV show "Twin Peaks," the main character Laura Palmer speaks in an unintelligible, supernatural tongue. The last episode leaves the viewers hanging (like an apple on a tree): Agent Cooper is possessed by the evil spirit Bob.
- Joe Biden was accused of plagiarizing a speech during his presidential run in 1988.
- The Magic Mountain is a novel by Thomas Mann that takes place at a sanatorium in Switzerland.
- According to many, the year of Creation was 4414 B.C. Perry supports teaching Creationism in schools.
- A study in May of 2012 announced results to support a theory that dinosaur flatulence emitted methane into the air and led to the species' extinction. The headline referred to was the real headline in Current Biology.
- Clint Eastwood did a (widely panned) skit at the 2012 Republican National Convention during which he talked to an empty chair—pretending Obama was sitting on it.

Democratic Primary

- Hillary Clinton's 2008 campaign TV ad was real. The line "It's 3 a.m...." is from the ad.
- Edward Snowden was a National Security Agency contractor who revealed that the NSA and Verizon were capturing Americans' cell phone data.
- "Play a nice game of Solitaire" is a line from "The Manchurian Candidate." Whenever the lead character hears this line, he becomes brainwashed, and his brainwashing leads him to commit murder.
- "Have you checked the children?" is a line from "When a Stranger Calls." In the movie the babysitter receives creepy phone calls from a killer—who it turns out is in the house with her.
- Philanthropist Chelsea Clinton married a wealthy investment banker and bought an apartment in Manhattan for $10.5 MM. "Moving On Up" is the theme song from the TV show "The Jeffersons."

- The actors listed as George Clooney supporters are really Democrats. The list is a spoof on the "Six Degrees of Kevin Bacon" game.
- Cary Grant was a secret homosexual who tried to cover it up by marrying and pretending to be straight. It was generally known in Hollywood that he was gay, and his peers helped keep it a secret to protect his career. There have been rumors that Clooney is pulling the same stunt.
- Before he was famous, Clooney had a role on "The Facts of Life" TV show as a handyman. Mrs. Garrett is a housemother in the show.
- Former Illinois governor Rob Blagojevich was wire-tapped and recorded as saying "I've got this thing and it's f***ing golden"—referring to his power to fill the Senate vacancy seat left by Obama. Willy Wonka is a storybook character that hides golden tickets into chocolate bars.

The Zeppo Marx Roast
- Zeppo Marx actually died in 1979. But had he lived he would have been 98 in 1999—the year Jon Stewart's "The Daily Show" launched.
- Marx is notoriously known as being the only Marx Brother of the four that was not at all funny. His brothers Groucho, Chico and Harpo were hilarious.
- In 2002, documentarian Michael Moore harshly interviewed then elderly actor Charlton Heston. Charleston Chew is a candy bar.

ART AND MONEY: CHAMPAGNE FINANCE
Chicago Billionaires OutsmART Chicago Mayor
- I mailed this version of *Grade A Papers* (as Volume 2) to The Griffins—a real billionaire couple in Chicago.
- Actor Vince Vaughn is a Republican from Chicago.
- The Chicago Art Institute houses Henri Matisse's "Bathers by a River" and Man Ray's "Chess Set." ("One Night in Bangkok" is a song from the musical "Chess.") Jackson Pollack was an abstract painter who has several of works displayed at the Chicago Art Institute. His paintings are intricate, incomprehensible and consist of chaotic lines, colorful swirls and frenetic strokes.
- The Griffins did donate $19 MM to the construction of the Art Institute's new modern wing in 2006.
- Mayor Rahm Emanuel spearheaded the effort to close 49 Chicago public schools in 2013.

Chicago Mayor OutsmARTS Chicago Billionaires
- I mailed this version of *Grade A Papers* (as Volume 3) to Chicago Mayor Rahm Emanuel.
- Ken Griffin is president of Citadel, a hedge fund company. CITGO is a gas station.
- Charles Lafitte Rosé is a cheap brand of champagne. Beaujolais—despite being celebrated in France as the year's first harvest—is (arguably) a poor wine.
- Anne Griffin is French. "872 North State Street just off the Red Line" is the address of "Frenchy's Adult Bookstore.
- Ken Griffin purchased the abstract painting "False Start" for $80 MM. It was painted by American contemporary artist Jasper Johns. "False Start" is an abstract mishmash of colors. The Abrakadoodle Art Studio for Kids is a real studio in Singapore where children take art classes.
- Actor Owen Wilson supported Hillary Clinton's presidential run in 2008. Wilson and Vaughn starred together in the movie "The Wedding Crashers."
- A famous Chicago statue is "Cloud Gate" in Millennium Park. However, it is widely known as "The Bean."
- The Smith Museum of Stained Glass is a real museum at Chicago's Navy Pier.

THE DEBATES
Mount Rushmore Face-Off
- In the mid-sixties, Mitt Romney attended Cranbrook Institute—a prep school for boys—in Michigan. When Romney was a student, he pinned down a boy who had long hair and cruelly cut it off.
- Obama gave a startlingly lackluster performance during his first debate against Romney in 2012. (Obama debated against John McCain in 2008.)
- In his book Dreams of My Father, Obama recalls "smoking pot in a van." A Staged Debate
- Actress Kim Cattrall lent her voice to a Manhattan GPS system—using the sexy voice of her character Samantha in the TV show "Sex and the City."
- Kraine Theater is a tiny, off-off-Broadway experimental theater in Manhattan.
- Jar Jar Binks is an annoying character from "Star Wars : The Clone Wars."
- Paul Ryan obsessively sipped water during his vice presidential debate against Biden in 2012. "
- …search party on a quest to save Ryan located him in private" sounds like "Saving Private Ryan."

STEWART'S INAUGURATION AND EXECUTIVE OUTFIT
The Assassination Attempt and the Spaceballs Alien
- Annie Leibovitz is a famous photographer. She and Stewart never married.
- In a contentious 2004 interview on the CNN news show "Crossfire," Stewart enraged host Tucker Carlson by calling Carlson out on "Crossfire's" biased, sensationalistic reporting. Carlson was 35 at the time and wore a bow tie. "Crossfire" was taken off the air shortly after the Stewart interview.
- Singer Janet Jackson alleges she experienced a "wardrobe malfunction" that revealed her breast at the XXXVIII Super Bowl Halftime Show.
- In the movie "Alien," an alien bursts out of actor John Hurt's character's stomach. In Mel Brooks' parody "Spaceballs," Hurt makes a guest appearance in a diner scene. In this scene, an alien bursts out of Hurt's stomach. The alien dons a top hat and cane and sings "Ragtime Gal" on the counter.

ROMANTIC ESCAPADES AND THE NSA
Colbert's Silent Tongue
- In the TV series "Downton Abbey," a character slips on a bar of soap to tragic results.
- Donald O'Connor and Gene Kelly starred in "Singing in the Rain." In this movie, their characters devise a scheme where an actress lip-synchs to the voice of another woman. In a famous scene the other woman stands behind as curtain as the actress pre-tends to sing on stage.
- Bill O'Reilly is a conservative political commentator who has appeared on "The Colbert Report." Colbert's mock persona on "The Colbert Report" is modeled after O'Reilly.

Stewart's Cabinet Unhinged
- Conan O'Brien did a skit where he pretend-ed to run across the country (from New York City to Los Angeles) to accept the job of "Late Night" host—replacing Jay Leno. Due to lackluster reviews, O'Brien only lasted seven months in the role.
- O'Brien, Stewart and Colbert once staged a mock feud: "Who Made Mike Huckabee."
- "Solo dad" sounds like "Soledad." Soledad O'Brien is a broadcast journalist unrelated to Conan.
- Cheatham County Community Theater is a real theater in Kingston Springs, Tennessee.
- Fresh Pond Mall is a real shopping center in Cambridge, Massachusetts.
- Dolly Parton played a secretary in "9 to 5" which takes place in New York City.
- "Dear Abby" is an advice column.

- Elle Décor is a home décor company.
- Miss Daisy is a character in the movie "Driving Miss Daisy," in which she is driven around by a chauffeur.
- Jack Sparrow is the name of the lead pirate character in "Pirates of the Caribbean."
- John McCain served in Vietnam. He had an affair during his first marriage.
- Demeter—in Greek Mythology—is Goddess of the Harvest. For six months each year, her beloved daughter is imprisoned in the Underworld. In grief, Demeter neglects the harvest during these six months each year—causing winter. She returns to the harvest when she has her daughter back.

Samantha's Bees and John's Olives
- Best Buy's (an appliance store) technical support team is called "The Geek Squad." Bed, Bath and Beyond is a retail store.
- Vladimir Putin passed a law in December 2012 that prohibits Americans from adopt-ing children in Russia.
- You can only get to Kamchatka, Russia by sea or air.
- "Please Sir, I want some more" is a line from the book Oliver Twist—which is a tale about an English orphan named Oliver.
- Miss Hannigan is the mean proprietor of an orphanage in the musical "Annie." In one scene she pours gin into her bathtub.

The Incorporation of Congress and the Inferiority Complex of the SEC
- "Occupy Wall Street" was a protest movement. "Wall Street: Money Never Sleeps" was a sequel to the movie "Wall Street" starring Michael Douglas as Gordon Gekko.

The Sexting Scandal of Petraeus and Paula
- Former CIA Director David Petraeus had an affair with his biographer, Paula Broadwell (not Paula Abdul the singer).
- Petraeus and Broadwell would jog together in Afghanistan (not rollerblade).
- John Inglis (not Linglis) is Director of the NSA.

E-Dating Hackers Spread Virus
- President George W. Bush claimed there were weapons of mass destruction.
- The quotes about Mercury poisoning are real from online forums.
- Hermes is a messenger in Greek Mythology who delivers messages between the Gods and the Mortals. Hermes is known as Mercury in Roman Mythology.
- "It's Just Lunch" (not "It's Just Punch") is a real dating service that arranges for singles to meet face-to-face for lunch.

GLOBAL FRICTION AND OTHER TALES OF DISASTER

The Amazon Plant Invasion
- The notion of man-eating plants comes from the show "Little Shop of Horrors." In this musical, Venus flytrap-like plants consume and conquer earth.
- There is a song in the musical called "Don't Feed the Plants."

An Infestation of Tics Down Under
- "The Wiggles" is a musical group that per-forms kids songs. They have a song called "Big Red Car." In their official music video, Jeff Fratt (one of "The Wiggles") falls asleep in the back seat.
- Tony Abbott is the Prime Minister of Australia. Elvis Costello (singer) sounds like Abbott and Costello (vaudeville duo).

McDonalds Serves Freedom Flies
- In 2003 U.S. officials renamed "French Fries" to "Freedom Fries" in three Congressional cafeterias in protest against France's opposition to the War in Iraq.
- "The Mold War" sounds like "The Cold War."
- In 2013, McDonalds' salads only made up to 3 percent of all orders.
- Joan of Arch sounds like Joan of Arc, the French folk heroine.
- The Study Abroad Tax Evasion Scandal
- Hofbräuhaus, Brasserie Julien and Restaurante Figueira Rubaiyat are famous restaurants in Germany, France and Brazil.
- 餓 孩 in 香 means "Starving Children" in "China."

The Clothing of Guantanamo
- Actress Sigourney Weaver battles in mechanical robot gear in "Aliens." Weaver also starred in "Ghost Busters." In "Ghost Busters" the Stay Puft Marshmallow Boy terrorizes New York City.

Italy Loses Color
- San Marino and the Vatican City are independent cities states—they are not considered a part of Italy despite their being landlocked by it. (Sicily and Sardinia are parts of Italy.)
- Frederico Fellini was an Italian director whose films include "8 1/2" and "La Dolce Vita"—two black and white art films in the 1960s.

The Controversial Erection of the BOLLYWOOD Sign in Tirumala
- Director Danny Boyle directed "Trainspotting" and "Slum Dog Millionaire."
- The child actors in "Slum Dog Millionaire" were poorly compensated despite the film's success.
- "Good Will Bunting" sounds like "Good Will Hunting"—a movie by director Gus Van Sant.
- "Boost" is a popular chocolate-flavored beverage kids drink in India.

The Rise and Fall of the White Bread Factory: Cutting Off The Trust
- No Cheeps.

DOMESTICATED NUISANCES AND A CRAZY LITTLE THING CALLED WAR

Giving America the New Bird
- Brenda Starr is a comic book character—a glamorous, redheaded investigative reporter.
- The journal quotes about the African Grey Parrot are legit.

Fraggles Fuss About Fracking
- Stewart really did appear as a guest on "Sesame Street" and Miss Piggy really did drop by "The Daily Show."
- HBO and CBC were the two cable channels that carried "Fraggle Rock."

The Mississippi Missile Crisis
- "An officer and a gentlewoman" sounds like the movie "An Officer and a Gentleman."
- Aruba rhymes with Cuba.

A Crockpot of Bull and the Texas Secession
- 25,000 signatures are needed in order for the Federal Government to respond to a petition. Texas's petition to secede from the U.S. exceeded the 25,000 mark in 2012.
- Thomas Edison owned the "Electric Light Company" (not the "Electric Write Company").
- San Antonio and Austin are democratically leaning cities in a staunchly Republican state.
- "Embrace puns and clay pigeons" sounds like "embrace guns and religion."
- Waxy O'Connor's is a real Irish Pub on the Riverwalk in San Antonio.

- "Austin City Limits" is a famous radio show.
- Davy Crockett (not Crocker) did not marry Betty Crocker. Betty Crocker is not even a real person, but an American icon for baking. "...married baker Betty" sounds like "Mary Baker Eddy"—the founder of Christian Science.

The Perfume Wars
- The Swiss are known for being neutral—not opinionated.

HEALTH AND EPIDEMICS
The Whore on Drugs
- The Palmer family's chef is really rumored to be the inventor of the brownie.
- Bertha Palmer's husband's first name is Potter.
- Auguste Rodin's famous sculpture is "The Kiss" (not "The Genital Kiss"). Rodin sculpted dogs, but not humping dogs.
- Rodin actually did sculpt Bertha Palmer, but not in the likeness of a headless bust.
- Sculptress Camille Claudel was Rodin's lover. She was very jealous—but her jealousy was over other women, not who sculpted them.
- "Fear and loafing for lost wages" sounds like Fear and Loathing in Las Vegas—a book about strung out road-trippers.

The Regeneration of the Smartphone into the Human Hand
- The first smartphone was really named Simon. It was invented by IBM in 1992. Ac-cording to USA Today, "IBM borrows twice as much money as it earns annually."
- There is an old superstition that if you drop a fork, it means someone is coming to visit.
- Daniel Day Lewis is an acclaimed actor who possesses a unique ability to play dramatically different roles. He starred in the movie "My Left Foot."

The Long Term Effects of Lasik Come to Light
- May 13 is singer Stevie Wonder's birthday.
- Both Wonder and Ray Charles are blind. Charles is more highly respected as a serious musician than Wonder.
- The whites of the eyes are called "sclera," not "scareras."
- The highest note ever sung was by Maria Aloysia Antonia Weber in Mozart's "Popoli di Tessaglia" concerto in 1777.

AN ECONOMIC COLLAPSE AND ITS NIPPLE EFFECT
- The lead male character in the movie "Boogie Nights" is well-endowed.
- The biggest layoffs during the Recession included General Motors, City Group, Merrill Lynch and JP Morgan Chase.
- There were 9,177,877 whites living in Illinois according a 2012 census.

Obama-Éclair (The Affordable Heath Bar Act) and the Smithsonian Sweet Tooth
- On June 28, 2012 the Supreme Court held up the statute for the Affordable Care Act.
- "A movable sweet" sounds like "a movable feast."
- American business owners with more than 49 employees must provide health care benefits.
- Diana Ross was the lead singer of "The Supremes" girl group. Another girl group during the same era was "Candy and the Kisses."
- In 1981, Sandra Day O'Connor became the first woman appointed to the Supreme Court.
- Actress Sharon Stone plays a character in "Basic Instinct" who grabs the attention of her interrogators by uncrossing her legs to show she's not wearing underwear.

THE PRESIDENTS PLAYHOUSE

The White House is a Fun House: From Remote Control Drones to "Being John Edwards"

- "Yes, We Can" was Obama's campaign slogan during his 2008 presidential run.
- During his presidency, Ronald Reagan launched the Strategic Defense Initiative, which was also known as Star Wars. It was an anti-ballistic missile defense program that was set up in 1984.
- David Axelrod was a presidential advisor to Obama. Axl Rose was the lead singer of "Guns n' Roses."
- In Oscar Wilde's novel The Picture of Dorian Gray, a portrait of the protagonist ages, but the protagonist does not. He watches himself get older in the painting; although in "real life" he does not age throughout the years.
- In the movie "Being John Malkovich," people crawl through a portal into actor Malkovich's brain. They co-exist in Malkovich's brain and body. John Edwards, former senator and vice presidential candidate, has a sordid past of infidelity and smarminess.

The Presidents Playhouse: A Cellar Discovery

- On June 11, 1962 Frank Morris (with two other prisoners) escaped from Alcatraz by chipping away at his jail cell wall with tools—creating a secret passage he crawled through.
- There is a contemporary classical composer named John Adams. He composed an opera called "Nixon in China."
- Former White House intern Monica Lewinsky fooled around with a cigar under Bill Clinton's watchful guard.
- Spiro Agnew was disbarred.
- Millard Fillmore started the White House library.
- Harvey Milk was gay. Barbara Pierce Bush is gay.
- Franklin Delano Roosevelt used a wheelchair. Andrew Jackson used a hickory cane.
- Actress Marilyn Monroe sang seductively to John F. Kennedy on his 45th birthday.
- Richard Nixon lied like Pinocchio. Clinton plays the sax.
- In 1992 Dan Quayle misspelled potato on TV.
- Lincoln was assassinated at a theater.
- Warren G. Harding gambled away White House china in a poker game.
- Ronald Reagan loved jelly beans.
- "I would gladly pay you Tuesday for a hamburger today" is a line from the Popeye comic strip and movie. It's spoken by Wimpy—a portly (like Taft) scam artist.
- "Harlequin Head" is a painting by Picasso that was stolen.
- Andy Warhol featured unopened soup cans in his paintings.
- A chaise lounge is part of the action in director Stanley Kubrick's "Eyes Wide Shut" orgy scene.
- Grover Cleveland got married in the White House.
- Woodrow Wilson ratified the 19th amendment —allowing women the right to vote.
- Theodore Roosevelt—a conservative—was nonetheless an avid supporter of labor unions.
- Former French Prime Minister Francois Mitterrand openly split his time between his wife and his mistress.
- Michael Dukakis ran unsuccessfully for president in 1988.
- Actor Dennis Haysbert played a U.S. president in the TV series "24."
- King George VI suffered from a bad stutter, which was most pronounced when he delivered public speeches.
- Stewart says a lot of swear words that get bleeped out on TV.

Life After Laughs

- Pee-Yew Research Center sounds like Pew Research Center.

OFFICE OF THE MAYOR
CITY OF CHICAGO

RAHM EMANUEL
MAYOR

August 7, 2014

Ms. Elizabeth Schaefer
Books on a Whim
Post Office Box 5066
Evanston, Illinois 60204

Dear Ms. Schaefer:

Please accept my sincere gratitude and appreciation for your book *Grade A Papers*. This gift is being graciously accepted on behalf of the City and will be recorded in the official Mayoral Gift Log.

Thank you for your support and I extend my best wishes for much continued success.

Sincerely,

Rahm Emanuel
Mayor

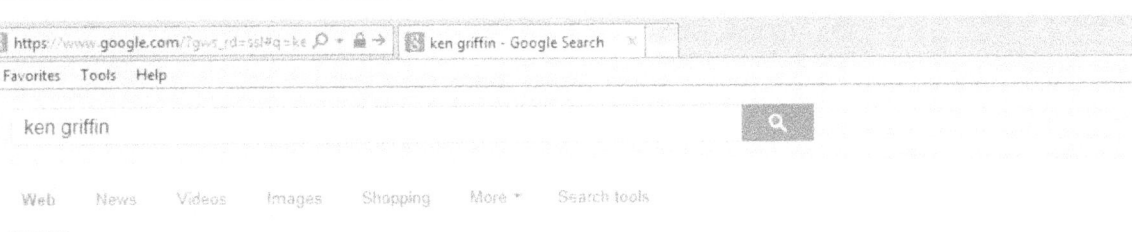

ken griffin

Web News Videos Images Shopping More ▾ Search tools

About 4,310,000 results (0.30 seconds)

Ken Griffin Parodies - booksonawhim.com
www.booksonawhim.com/
Funny coffeetable books with art plus political & celebrity jokes

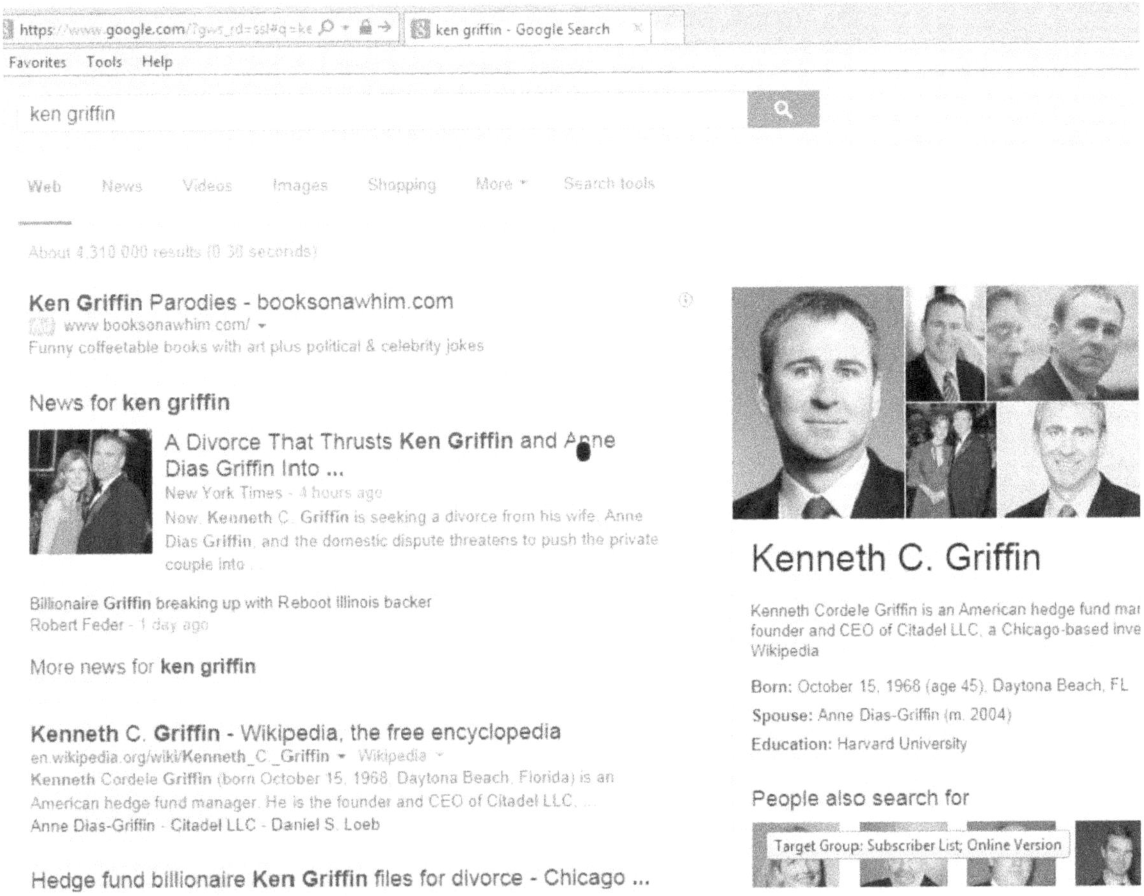

News for **ken griffin**

A Divorce That Thrusts **Ken Griffin** and Anne Dias Griffin Into ...
New York Times - 4 hours ago
Now, Kenneth C. Griffin is seeking a divorce from his wife, Anne Dias Griffin, and the domestic dispute threatens to push the private couple into ...

Billionaire **Griffin** breaking up with Reboot Illinois backer
Robert Feder - 1 day ago

More news for **ken griffin**

Kenneth C. Griffin - Wikipedia, the free encyclopedia
en.wikipedia.org/wiki/Kenneth_C._Griffin ▾ Wikipedia
Kenneth Cordele **Griffin** (born October 15, 1968, Daytona Beach, Florida) is an American hedge fund manager. He is the founder and CEO of Citadel LLC, ...
Anne Dias-Griffin - Citadel LLC - Daniel S. Loeb

Hedge fund billionaire **Ken Griffin** files for divorce - Chicago ...

Kenneth C. Griffin

Kenneth Cordele Griffin is an American hedge fund man founder and CEO of Citadel LLC, a Chicago-based inve
Wikipedia

Born: October 15, 1968 (age 45), Daytona Beach, FL
Spouse: Anne Dias-Griffin (m. 2004)
Education: Harvard University

People also search for

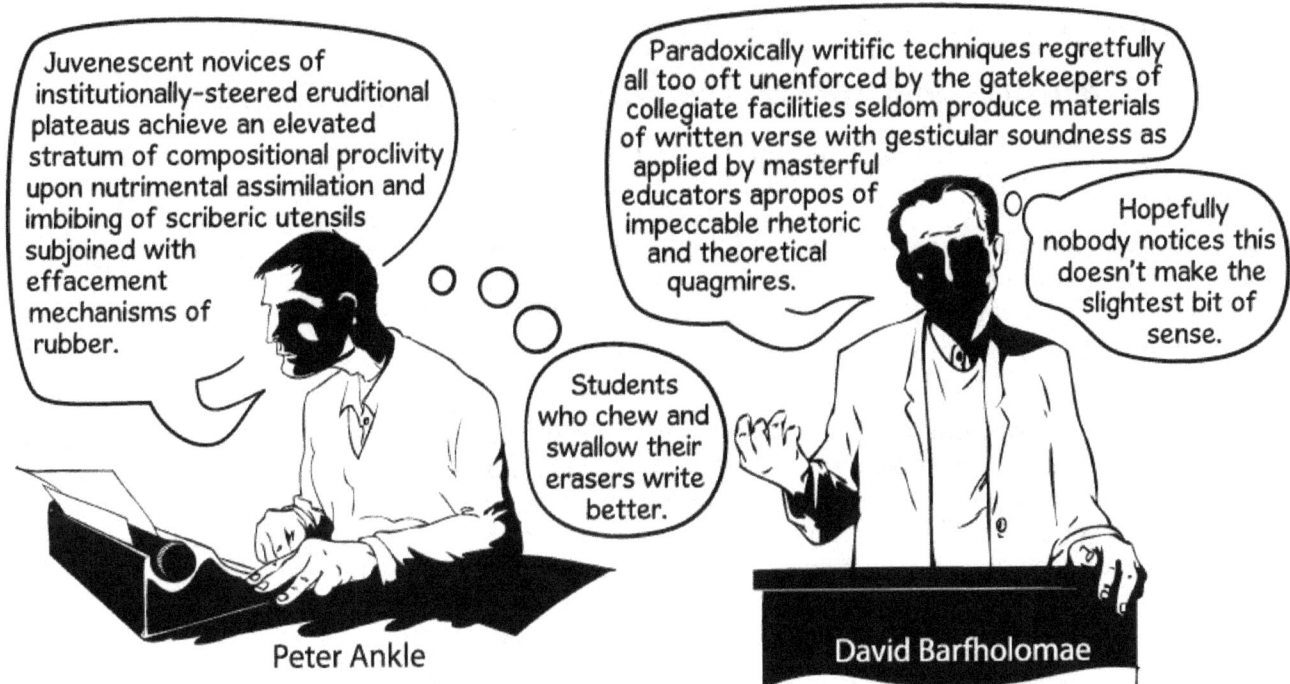

COMPOSITION THEORIST PARODIES

Make No Room for Kids: Bells Ding for Online Classes K-8
An Argumentative Abstract by Richard Fukerson
Sponsored by The University of Phonics

Any pedagogical theory, irregardless of its self-aggrandizing maker, that enlists the nerve to counter the ground breaking, earth shattering eruditional philosophy about to be put forth, is by any definition, a vainglorious, foolhardy soul, forever lost in the woods of antiquated methods and prehistoric deliverance.

My lengthy, long-winding path of research, dating back to my childhood composition studies at the playground for precocious tots—whereon I conjugalmated verbs with mothers on chalk—to my locker room argotic antics at the junior school of higher education wherein I swept my finger on shower doors punctuating steam—my portfolii of reconnoitering writifical exploration qualifies me to proclaim the following findings a truth: worthy of regulatory application and subsequent penalization for neglect to comply.

The very nature of my familiarity with youthful scribe commissions me to spew unto the reader cataclysmal residuals of my mental precocity. The matter about which I am about to urp forth, complexicated a vast mass of field research, Internet analytics, laborious child interviews, consultations with sponsor marketers, and my own frequently untapped thought machine.

Early speakers of the English language colonized America in the late 15_{th} century. [This was quite controversial in the youths' native England when their parents learnt of it. Colonization was widely unperformed in Europe and at the time was a regimental induction isolated to recently birthed Jewish boys alone.] Their composition studies took place in quaint schoolhouses and makeshift tree houses. According to termite-unscathed, sap-preserved writings on the walls, arboreal chirographic experts surmise that children learned composition by means of tapping their pencils into their papers like pointillism or medieval drills.

This tapping method evolved and mutated into strokes and lines, into block letters and cursive. The direness to modify ones elementary exercises to divert time lapses and modernity breaches is imperative to the transcendental regeneration of our offspring. Expedient evolution entails training and agreement to relinquish skeptics who disagree with us. Thus, civilized mankind must recognize that the time of the trained has arrived at the station.

In art and culture, schoolhouses have long been associated with warmth, with fuzzy feelings of goodness, with Popsicle stick crafts and storybook hours. The hardened cold truth is that the last Popsicle craft was built in 1983 by Miss Mayberry's 1_{st} grade class at Stony Lane Elementary School in North Kingstown, Rhode Island, and the last storybook hour assembled in 1957 in Miss Gertrude's 4_{th} grade class at The Good Shepherd School in Golden Valley, Minnesota.

Regretability—parental or unparental, pedagogue or apedagogue—may be arguable, but even the commonest of folk acquiesce that today's schoolhouse is a very different setting than it was in our day or back in 1492 when administrates mandated schoolgirls wear bonnets and schoolboys wear britches on premises.

Today, schoolhouse halls are rampant with terrors: Kindergartners wearing wash-on tattoos of violent arachnid and chiroptera superheroes; Second Graders lacing paper airplanes with postage stamps as passenger windows; Fifth Graders thinking juice cocktail is 100% juice; 7th Graders at lunch snorting boiled spaghetti noodles up their nostrils; and 8th Graders hole-punching their ear lobes and sticking titanium studs through the punctured flesh.

As educators, it is time to collect ourselves, reassemble and evolve. An overwhelming influx of A's supports that online college programs are the most efficacious vehicles for college students' academic enrichment and their parents'. We have tested the waters: It is time to integrate online education for grades K—8.

Hereith beneath I plant the curricular seed for the nearith forthcoming of juvenescence education as I foresee it:

THE PROGRAM

School Schedules

The children's daily schedules need not differ dramatically from a "normal" school day. Children will rise to their wake up call; march to breakfast and plop before the television set; perfunctorily dress (in school uniforms if an ecclesiastical institute); groom themselves with comb, brush, and toothpaste; bundle up if it's brisk; step out the front door; close the door; count to ten; open the door; enter back into the house; and fire up the computer.

Class will commence strictly at 9:00 am with the young students logging on with their unique User Identification (ID) and Password (PSWD) identifying themselves as present. (Students who log on late will be added to a tardy list. Students who sign on tardy more than three times a school year are subjected to stringent parental controls.)

A Glimpse at Curricula

Young grade school children will finger-paint on touch screen monitors; make collages of stock art in design programs; learn how to type lowercase letters by releasing the CAPS LOCK; and insert shapes like block arrows and flowcharts from word processing programs to evince geometrical grasp. (Hand-washing after using the bathroom will be based on the honor system. If suspicion of deceit is overt, keyboard swab tests will be executed.)

Older grade school children will practice their cursive by sweeping or swiping their computer mouse without lifting a finger; multiply and divide by learning how to copy and paste formulas into spreadsheets that generate the solutions; "Like" social media social studies; and author book reports upon perusing tabletified Electronic-books to minimize risk of paper cuts.

Middle school children will take timed placement tests that—by means of asterisks (SHIFT 8)—emulate the format of filling in dots with #2 lead pencil (an eraser will symbolically manifest itself in the form of a DEL key); dissect virtual harlequin frogs from The Sims: Endangered Animals PC game; learn Spanish and sex ed simultaneously by watching You Tubular media files of Diego Animal Rescuer Wears Deodorant and Starts Shaving; and ingest English Lit by listening to audio books of Great Expectations and A Brave New World.

A Highschool Reflection: At this point in continuance, I do not advocate the integration of high school curricula into a purely online format. By eliminating the face-to-face interplay between high school students, the young adults lose the confines in which to meet like-minded, able-bodied peers and lose their virginity—a critical maneuver in the everlasting existence of mankind. Granted, pundits of Medicine & Technology predict scientists will invent an electronic means for virginity forfeiture by path of simulation before college—and even possibly at the same time. (Soon enough we'll be growing babies in our gardens, and sexual intercourse will be a mere historical notion. Stories Grampa will tell your kids.)

Keeping in the Fun

Skeptics may scoff that school needs peppy, interactive activities to keep children's minds fresh, alert and percolating new brain cells. However, online elementary and middle school classes will integrate fun into formula . Just as in a normal school day, kids will enjoy Physical Education (P.E.). Modern technology has enabled computer users to interact—in real time—across a multitude of virtual sports platforms—from soccer to table tennis to fencing. With online P.E. there's no such thing as seasonal sports. Kids can play beach volleyball in the winter! (Middle school females enduring menstruation may eschew that week's activities by e-mailing the instructor a "." with scanned forensic sample.)

Choir, band, and drama are actionable with online schooling. Children rehearse via webcasts, and come recital time, parents are invited to their own home to login and listen to their child perform in synch with the other munchkinesqually groomed voices. Plays will be video-recorded for parents who come home late.

Extracurricular activities will be proffered such as fantasy football club; Google search races; classical keyboard lessons; Smartphone photography; field trips to online libraries; and Yearbook Club for blue screen class pictures.

Demographic Considerations and Controversies

Social interactional ostracization and hectoring will be an affliction of the past. With online classes, there will be no wedgies; no double dog dares or pulling hair; and no playground bullies. It is infeasible bullying be conducted via data processing machines; online bullying is a concept so impracticable that I employed zero research on the matter. Pushing a classmate's face off your screen will do nothing but break your computer; and kids needn't wear underwear when in attendance.

What about different demographic conditions (i.e., home lifestyle and ecopsycholoracential influencers)? Some children will have access to a grand patio sunroom with ergonomically crafted ottomans and wrist pads. While other children will be stationed in a windowless corners sitting stone cold on hard wooden benches or rocks. The privileged minorities' rooms will consistently sustain a comfy 72°F while other minorities' rooms will vacillate between a chilly 66 or a balmy 88. Propitiously, technology is ever-evolving: It be a "know brainer" that visionary inventors will engineer temperature-modifiable laptop speakers, wall breaker Windows, and comfy heated mouse pads large enough for the less fortunate children to snuggle into.

Composition theorist James Irving Berlin, states forth in his essay, "Rhetoric and Climatology in the Writing Class" that pupils cannot compositionally articulate their ideological values freely in stodgy, sterile classroom environments. I accede with this mindset. However, Berlin contends students need a wet environment to feel fresh to work well and expound. Now, that could be an electrical hazard for an online class—In particular, the cases where wireless access abstinence and unaffordability be employed. Therefore, I incline the reader to repel Berlin's fanciful notions about the wet part.

Theorist Good Lad Tobin approaches demographic inequalities from a famine-for-knowledge stance. In his essay "Eating Students, Eating Ourselves: Digesting the Teacher's Role in the Writing Class," he writes "Rhetorical sophistication is attainable by means of consuming students' minds without the theatrics of self-obsession." Tobin preaches that a teacher should be in close proximity to his student to consume ideas without bias. This is a laughable notion. Children are equally rechargeable batteries, and by 2028 teachers are all going to be robots anyway.

Can We Trust Them?

Opponents of online learning for K-8 cite the lack of parental whereabouts when the child is "attending" school à la maison. Working parents will not be at home to supervise the child, and stay-at-home parents—contrary to the moniker—have secret lives and don't really stay at home. Opponents voice fatiguing concerns for the children, indicating poor nutrition ("Children will eat cookies for lunch," they say); safety ("Children will find the hidden stash of detergent bullets and figure out how to load the dishwasher and chute"); and lack of discipline and Vitamin D.

Some opposing parents argue that their child will hibernate their computer as soon as the parents leave the house, and subject themselves to brain deadening, addictive soap operas marathons. Others argue their kid will get hooked on online video game playing—subsequently unable to shut down in the rare-but-precious moments when the family is home together for a sit-down dinner.

These absurd terrors are ludicrous and unfounded; the opposition's arguments are sheer non-profit anti-disbandment propaganda and a hush hush conspiracy steered by the Parent-Teacher Association (PTA). The PTA, dating back to its founding in 1897, has undeviatingly interfered in the schooling and scholarship of hundreds of millions of afore-potentialed children by corrupting their blank slates with huggy nurturing and community fostering as opposed to where the focus should be, which is on the wisdom imparted solidaritously by degreed Instructor.

I once referred to theorist Peter Ankle as an "Aristotle in modern dress." Yet, such a label better applies to yours truly. I, an educator, applaud online learning, and you parents, most likely are not teachers. "Those who educate children well are more to be honored than they who produce them; for these only gave them life, those the art of living well." In other words, I, Richard Fukerson, too wear woman's clothing.

Where Do We Go from Here?

This is another advantage of online schooling. We don't go anywhere.

Read Fukerson's full report "Make No Room for Kids: Bells Ding for Online Classes K-8" at Yale University's Beinecke Rare Book and Manuscript Library in New Haven, CT. The report is available in hard back only.

This work was sponsored by the University of Phonics, an innovative institution about to launch an exciting program for grades K-8, which, in the words of renowned composition theorist John Fukerson, Emeritus Texas A & M University, "An overwhelming influx of A's supports that on-line…programs are the most efficacious vehicles for…students' academic enrichment and their parents'."

If you would like to enroll your child in a trial run of a school year online, fill out the application downloadable at howtogofarwithoutgoinganywhereatall.com and mail it to 3157 E. Elwood St. 85034 with a signed mental liability release form.

```
This paper appears in Grade A Papers: The Slap Stack and accompanies three addi-
tional composition theorist parodies. Book is available booksonawhim.com.
```

Simon Simon
U.S. History of the Human Spirit
Professor Edgar Wombat

Whimsor College course

My Flesh is my Blanket Inside which I Hide

When I signed up for this class I thought it was a class on U.S. history of spirituality like when Christ got citizenship. I was excited to learn how he walked in American shoes as far back as when he didn't have any but sandals. I learned too late that this class is on the history of U.S. people who fought hardships with energy and determination. Here goes anyway.

Scott's Early Years

My selected past human for this assignment is Francis Scott Key. Scott was born in 1779 on a plantation called Terra Ruby. This means "earth of rubies". His birth was a messy birth which stained the cotton.

In junior high Scott joined the American Bible Society who congregated in the gymnasium on snowdays. He and his fellows petitioned the school library to extend book checkout due dates for *The Bible*. (I don't know if they won. I didn't finish that chapter in Scott's biography because my book was due back. If I had checked out *The Bible,* that would have been a clue.)

The Society petitioned to translate *The Bible* into Bantu with <u>no</u> due date. Here's why. So emancipated foreignly-fathered readers can check it out for free, and because <u>they</u> are free, they can move back to West Central Africa without worrying about late fees that would keep them in U.S. where guilt lacks conscience. Scott met Mary his wife at a rally.

Scott's Determination

Scott went to law school to pursue injustice legally. Following graduation Scott became an ambulance chaser with horses during the War of 1812. Scott lost his shame at the Battle of Baltimore. Here's how come. He wrote an epithet on a love letter as he watched the battle at Fort McHenry. The battle left 24 wounded and Scott chased none of their carts. When he prosecuted President Andrew Jackson's assassin in 1835, Scott's credibility plummeted when Jackson died of tuberculosis in 1845.

That's when Scott gave up his legit calling to follow his true calling: **hypocrisy.** In the 1800s' hypocrisy ranted rampant. Scott was a pioneer in good centurial company. Here's who.

- Take President Chester A. Arthur, executer of the Chinese Exclusion Act (1882) which kept Chinese people from entering U.S. on grounds of lack of respect for disobeying laws such as the Chinese Exclusion Act (1882).
- Take the Southern Activists who (unsuccessfully) pressured the Feds to purchase Cuba from Spain (1898) in order to ship slaves there from off American grounds on the grounds of American expansionism.

- Take publisher Joseph Pulitzer for (successfully) soliciting funds from the poor (1884) for the construction of the Statue of Liberty which symbolized illumination of independence on the grounds that shaded the ghettos.
- Take Edward Clarke, Harvard Professor, who—on grounds of mankind's survival—claimed (1873) that women who attend college grow bigger brains which destroys their wombs and quashes their reproductive abilities to produce boys.

These grand, progressive, early thinkers thought ahead of their times. They set the stage for 20th century despots like: Emma Goldman, womens' rights activist who opposed the womens' suffrage movement. President Eisenhower, who gave the executive order that gays in Federal Government may be dismissed for their inclinations in the name of ethical employment. Senator Joseph McCarthy who blacklisted Americans as a function of the House Committee of Un-American Activities. President John F. Kennedy, supporter of the U.S. Army School of the Americas' torture training curriculum with the aim of peacekeeping.

Like these standup gents and an activist, Scott made no excuses—stoking his own hypocrisy; and making it his own by means of poetry as a method. Mounting insurmountable barriers, Scott composed the time of his life.

Scott's Barrier

There is an Arlington elementary that sells Francis Scott Key blankets. It's a school and they're embroidered. They cost $25 if you round up or $24 if you round down. That's in Virginia. The blankets merchandise denotes a barricade of cold force. Here's how so.

Scott was the force behind the cold force. In arms with intimidation and degradation, he barricaded the brave with his body of beliefs. This was 19th century Ano Domini.

The brave heaved and pressed against the relentless cold to reach the early light. They marched as far as they could push against Admiral Beaufort's storm gale force on the empirical ruler. These wind gusts blew between the tears of Scott's sail, September 15, 1814

Scott's sail was like this analogy. A single feather with splayed down or a fine tooth comb with toothpick fangs spread open like legs. Scott was tickled to be a spectator of the Sisyphus crew from the canopied chambers of his ship. Scott watched the Maryland shenanigans with bemusement and poignancy because he was an aspiring poet.

Entertainers are generally exempt from dirtying their hands in battle. Take Ted Nugent: "So I got my notice to be in the draft. Do you think I was gonna lay down my guitar and go play army?" Take Phil Ochs: "I wish you well, Sarge, give 'em Hell! Kill me a thousand or so." Scott was the Nugent and Ochs of America's Hell Epoch.

He conquered the barrier of the brave through verse.

Scott was more than a poet. Scott was a conductor. Scott's baton was his blanket. Scott carried it streaming; he slept in it wet. Scott lugged it from war; he snuggled tight into it at night. Scott craved it with all his might; he waved it with a flick of his wrist. Scott slit it with a stick of fire; and used it to fan hostility.

When a man's blanket is stripped from him, he is skinned, and that's entertainment. Scott bundled up to enjoy the uncivil British battle line through a lyrical lens—magnificently magnified and exploited.

When his ditty was done, Scott hoisted his blanket up the mast, and invited America to glare at its blare. This is a hero in America. Here's more and then some song.

Scott's Victory

Francis Scott Key to his America:
"Are you willing, gentlemen, to abandon your country, to permit it to be taken from you, and occupied by the abolitionist, according to whose taste it is to associate and amalgamate with the Negro?" – Francis Scott Key, Writer, Star Spangled Banner

The Star Spangled Banner, 1814

Oh, say can you see by the dawn's early light
"It is not light that we need, but fire; it is not the gentle shower, but thunder. We need the storm, the whirlwind, and the earthquake". – Frederick Douglass

What so proudly we hailed at the twilight's last gleaming?
"Having soon discovered to be great, I must appear so, and therefore studiously avoided mixing in society, and wrapped myself in mystery". – Nat Turner

Whose broad stripes and bright stars thru the perilous fight,
*"An American, a Negro...two souls, two thoughts, two unreconciled strivings; two warring ideals in one dark body, whose dogged strength alone keeps it from being torn asunder".
– W.E.B. Dubois*

O'er the ramparts we watched were so gallantly streaming?
"Political life in our country has plowed in muddy channels, and needs the infusion of clearer and cleaner waters". – Frances Harper

And the rocket's red glare, the bombs bursting in air,
"I shall allow no man to belittle my soul by making me hate him". – Booker T. Washington

Gave proof through the night that our flag was still there.
"Every people should be originators of their own destiny". – Martin Delany

Oh, say does that star-spangled banner yet wave
"I done but do my duty boys. The flag never touched the ground.". – William Carney

O'er the land of the free and the home of the brave?
"I had crossed the line. I was free; but there was no one to welcome me to the land of freedom. I was a stranger in a strange land." – Harriet Tubman

On the other side of paradise

I got this far in the book: Scott is related to another F. Scott—the *Great Gatsby* writer which is about a very rich man. Bloodline is always an indicator. It proves creativity runs through the vain. Human bloodline traces back to Adam, a pure American. If not in the flesh, then in spirit.

This is a sneak peek at one of many fake student papers that will appear in *Grade A Papers II: A Funny Coffee Table Book for History Teachers and the Universe*. [Release slated 2015.] Visit booksonawhim.com.

Ebert Cog
Dean of Whimsor

Steffi Staff
Administrative Assistant

Whimsor History Department
Faculty

Vander Bleek
Department Chair

"Contemporary American History"
"History Through the Times"

Daphne Duck

"History of the Heart in Seoul"
"The Majestic History of Whimsor"

Chester Matted

"Modern Marvels: How Our Pasts Open Up Our Presents"
"Let's Backtrack (Workshop)"

Holly Golly

"Domestic Traumas on Foreign Soils"
"The History That Doesn't Matter"

Molly Golly

"Foreign Traumas on Domestic Soils"
"The History That Matters"

Ned Nappy

"World History in America"
"The European Influence and Other Obscenities"

Rhonda Rhodehouse
(Adjunct)
"American Melodrama"

Stellan Scotchguard

"American Inventions"
"The Industrious Revolution"

Edgar Wombat

"U.S. History of the Human Spirit"
"The War of the Worlds Wise Webs"

booksonawhim.com

Whimsor College

Whimsor College breaks earth in 2015. Whimsor is an imaginary liberal arts college, wherein wacky, wonderful students and teachers take place.

Whimsor is nestled inside the Wilshire Woods in Columbia, Missouri. This fictitious institution of higher learning is a mere two miles north of the city center—North of Shady Lake and East of Bear Creek Trail. Visit: booksonawhim.com/whimsor-college.html

About the author

Beth Schaefer is a new humorist and creator of Books on a Whim (dreamed up May 24, 2013 and incorporated July 23, 2013).

In addition to writing humorous books on a whim, Beth is a college English teacher and publisher.

Contact

Books on a Whim, Inc.
P.O. Box 5066
Evanston, IL 60204-5066
USA
www.booksonawhim.com
info@booksonawhim.com

Art credits

Front and back covers by Donna Harriman Murillo
White House column with stiletto by Dreamrise
Cheep Sheet graphic (egg with flag) by Julizar Hakim
Composition theorists graphic by Fabio Fantini
Whimsor History Department faculty by Fabio Fantini

www.ingramcontent.com/pod-product-compliance
Lightning Source LLC
Chambersburg PA
CBHW080449110426
42743CB00016B/3331